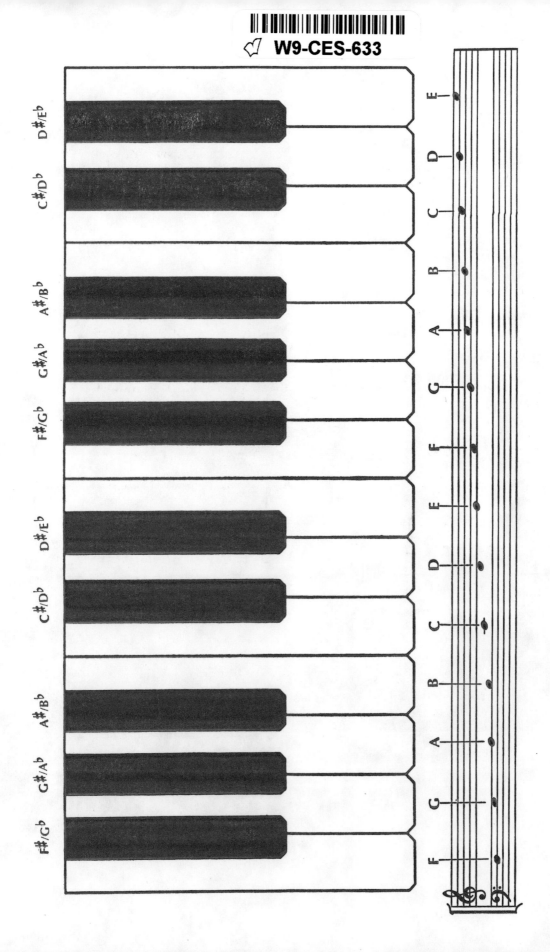

World of *Music*

Jane Beethoven • Jennifer Davidson
Catherine Nadon-Gabrion
Authors

Carmino Ravosa • Phyllis Weikart
Theme Musical   **Movement**

Darrell Bledsoe
Producer, Vocal Recordings

Silver Burdett & Ginn

Morristown, NJ • Needham, MA

Atlanta, GA • Cincinnati, OH • Dallas, TX • Menlo Park, CA • Deerfield, IL

ISBN 0-382-07049-6

Contents

Music for Living 2

Understanding Music 88

MUSIC FOR LIVING

Music in Your Life

Make a list of all the places where you might hear music during a single day. Then think about this question: What would your life be like without music?

What Would the World Be Like Without Music?

Words and Music by Doug Nichol

What would the world be like with-out mu-sic? Beau-ti-ful mu - sic.

Just think of what it means to you and me.

What would the world be like with-out mu - sic?

Try to i-mag-ine how emp-ty our lives would be.

There'd be no mel-o-dies __ to "whis-tle while you work."

There'd be no tunes to hum, __ mm, _____

There'd be no songs to sing __ to help you change the way you feel, __

D.C. al Fine

you'd have to find an-oth-er way. _____

Here is an excerpt from a song that you will find on page 226 in your book. Can you tell from the words how this song should be sung?

Lift Every Voice and Sing

Lift every voice and sing,
Till earth and heaven ring,
Ring with the harmonies of liberty;
Let our rejoicing rise,
High as the list'ning skies,
Let it resound loud as the rolling sea.

James Weldon Johnson

Outward Bound

Shanties were the work songs sung aboard sailing ships.
The shanteyman set the rhythm for the work with his solo.
Listen for the shanteyman's solo and join in on the chorus.

Feel the music swinging along—two beats to a measure.

Rio Grande

American Shantey

1. Oh say, were you ev - er in Ri - o Grande?
2. A jol - ly good ship and a jol - ly good crew,

A - way _____ for Ri - o!

It's there that the riv - er runs down gold - en sand,
A jol - ly good mate and a jol - ly good crew,

We are bound for Ri - o Grande! _____

REFRAIN

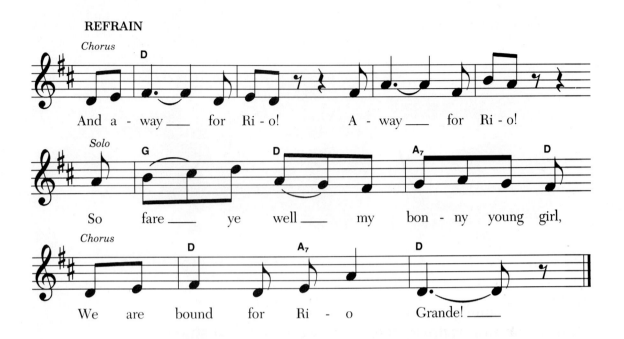

And a - way ___ for Ri - o! A - way ___ for Ri - o!

So fare ___ ye well ___ my bon - ny young girl,

We are bound for Ri - o Grande! ___

3. The anchor's aweigh and the sails they are set, . . .
   The gals that we're leaving we'll never forget, . . .
   Refrain

4. Goodbye to Sally and Sarah and Sue, . . .
   To all who are list'ning, it's goodbye to you, . . .
   Refrain

Four Patterns for Percussion

Choose a percussion instrument and play one of these
patterns to accompany "Rio Grande."

Can you play a different pattern for each verse of
the song?

An American Work Song

Many Irish immigrants found work laying the tracks of the first continental railroad. The Irish wit and love of singing helped the workers survive the hardships of their job.

As you listen to this Irish-American railroad song, tap or clap the steady beat. It will help you feel the rhythm that made the work a little easier.

Paddy Works on the Railway

Irish-American Railroad Song

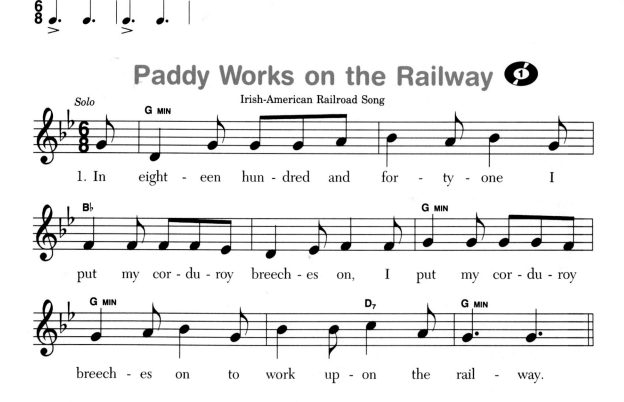

1. In eight - een hun - dred and for - ty - one I
put my cor - du - roy breech - es on, I put my cor - du - roy
breech - es on to work up - on the rail - way.

Chorus
REFRAIN

Fil - li - mee - oo - ree - oo - ree - ay, Fil - li - mee - oo - ree - oo - ree - ay,

Fil - li - mee - oo - ree - oo - ree - ay, To work up - on the rail - way.

2. In eighteen hundred and forty-two
I left the old world for the new,
Oh, spare me the luck that brought me through
To work upon the railway. *(Refrain)*

3. It's "Pat, do this," and "Pat, do that,"
Without a stocking or cravat,
And nothing but an old straw hat,
While working on the railway. *(Refrain)*

Add a Countermelody

Here is a countermelody to sing with the refrain of the song.

Countermelody (Refrain)

Fil - li - mee - oo - ree - oo - ree - ay, Fil - li - mee - oo - ree - oo - ree - ay,

Fil - li - mee - oo - ree - oo - ree - ay, Oo - ree - ay.____

A Folk Hero

John Henry, a legendary character, was the southern
steel-driving man whose fame spread across the country.

Sing this song as if you were telling a story. Let your voice
express the meaning of the words.

John Henry

Folk Song from Southern United States

1. When John Hen - ry ___ was just a lit - tle ba - by,
2. Well, the cap - tain ___ said to John ___ Hen - ry,

Sit - tin' on his dad - dy's knee,
"Gon - na bring that steam drill round,

He ___ gave one long and ___ lone - some cry,
Gon - na take that steam drill ___ out on the job,

Said, "A ham - mer be the death of me." me."
Gon - na whop that steel ___ on ___ down." down."

3. John Henry told his captain,
   "Well, a man ain't nothin' but a man,
   But before I let your steam drill beat me down,
   I'll die with a hammer in my hand." *(2 times)*

4. Oh, the man that invented the steam drill,
   He thought that he was mighty fine,
   But John Henry drove his steel fifteen feet,
   And the steam drill drove only nine. *(2 times)*

5. John Henry kept hammerin' on the mountain,
   There was lightnin' in his eye.
   He drove so hard that he broke his heart,
   And he laid down his hammer and he died. *(2 times)*

6. They carried him off to the graveyard,
   They buried him in the sand.
   And people came from near and far
   To praise that steel-drivin' man. *(2 times)*

Song of the Old West

In the early days of our country, cowboys spent much of their working time on horseback. In winter they took care of the cattle on the range. In spring they drove the cattle to market along trails that were long and dangerous. This song tells about one of those cowboys and his horse named Doney Gal.

Tap this pattern as you listen to "Doney Gal." The music on the recording will tell you how fast or slow (or at what tempo) you will tap.

$\begin{smallmatrix}3\\4\end{smallmatrix}$ ♩. | ♩. | ♩. | ♩. |

tap   tap   tap   tap

Doney Gal

Folk Song from Oklahoma

REFRAIN

We're a-lone, Do-ney Gal, in the wind and hail, ___

Got-ta drive those do-gies down the trail. ___

VERSE

1. We'll ride the range from sun to sun, For a
2. A cow-boy's life is a wea-ry thing, For it's

cow-boy's work is ___ nev-er done, He's
rope ___ and brand and ___ ride and sing; Yes,

up   and   gone   at   the   break   of   day,

day   or   night   in   the   rain   or   hail,   He'll

Driv - in' the do - gies on their wea - ry way.

stay with his do - gies out ___ on the trail.

3. We whoop at the sun and yell through the hail,
But we drive the poor dogies down the trail;
And we'll laugh at the storms, the sleet and snow,
When we reach the town of San Antonio.

Parts for Percussion

Play one of these parts to accompany "Doney Gal."

Low drum

Woodblock

Triangle

Autoharp strum

Thunder on the Rails

Everyone knew when the *Wabash Cannon Ball* was heading down the track. Follow the words as you listen to the song. Can you find the words that describe the sound of this mighty train?

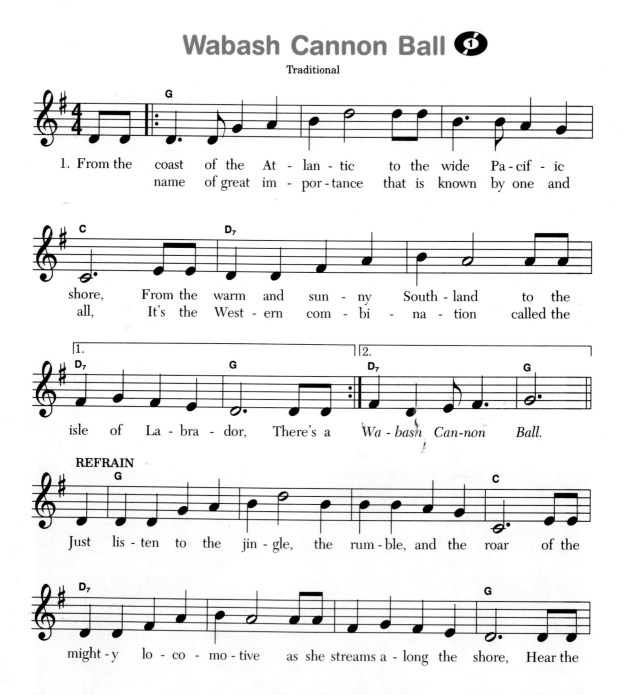

Wabash Cannon Ball

Traditional

1. From the coast of the At - lan - tic to the wide Pa - cif - ic
   name of great im - por - tance that is known by one and

   shore, From the warm and sun - ny South - land to the
   all, It's the West - ern com - bi - na - tion called the

   1. isle of La - bra - dor, There's a
   2. Wa - bash Can - non Ball.

REFRAIN

Just lis - ten to the jin - gle, the rum - ble, and the roar of the

might - y lo - co - mo - tive as she streams a - long the shore, Hear the

14

thun - der of the en - gine, hear the lone-some whis - tle call, It's the

West - ern com - bi - na - tion called the *Wa - bash Can-non Ball.*

2. There are cities of importance that are reached along the way,
    Chicago and Saint Louis and Rock Island, Santa Fe,
    And Springfield and Decatur and Peoria, Montreal,
    On the Western Combination called the *Wabash Cannon Ball.*

Chant-a-Pattern

The names of some of the cities mentioned in verse 2 of "Wabash Cannon Ball" are used in the chants below. While someone plays a steady beat on a woodblock, try chanting the patterns one after the other without missing a beat.

1. $\frac{4}{4}$
   Spring - field,   Spring - field

2. $\frac{4}{4}$
   Spring - field, De - ca - tur

3. $\frac{4}{4}$
   Rock   Is - land, Rock   Is - land

4. $\frac{4}{4}$
   Spring-field and Chi - ca - go

5. $\frac{4}{4}$
   Spring - field, Pe - o - ri - a

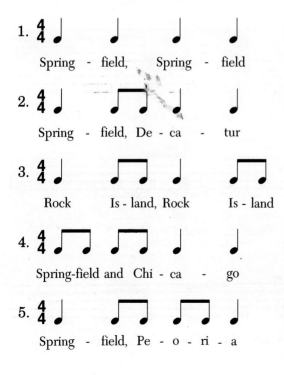

15

Song of the Canalers

The Erie Canal was opened in 1825. It provided an important link between the Great Lakes and the Atlantic Ocean.

As the barges moved along the canal, those on deck had to be cautious as they approached the bridges. What did they call out as a warning? You will find the answer in the words of this song.

Erie Canal

American Folk Song

1. I got a ___ mule, her name is ___ Sal,
2. Git up there, ___ Sal, we passed that ___ lock,

Fif - teen ___ miles on the E - rie Ca - nal! ___

She's a good old ___ work - er and a good old ___ pal,
And ___ we'll make ___ Rome ___ 'fore ___ six o' - clock,

Fif - teen ___ miles on the E - rie Ca - nal! ___

Solo

We've hauled some barg - es in our ___ day,
Just one more trip and in back we'll ___ go

Filled with lum - ber, coal, and ___ hay,
Through the rain and sleet and ___ snow,

And we know ev - 'ry inch of the way
'Cause we know ev - 'ry inch of the way

From Al - ba - ny ___ to ___ Buf - fa - lo ___

REFRAIN
Chorus

Low bridge, ev - 'ry - bod - y down,

Low bridge, 'cause we're com - ing to a town;

And you'll al - ways know your neigh - bor, You'll al - ways know your pal,

If you ev - er nav - i - gat - ed on the E - rie Ca - nal. ___

Song with a Catchy Rhythm

The rhythm of the words gives a catchy, off-balance movement to the music of this Black Spiritual. As you listen to the song, clap the steady beat or try this tap-clap pattern.

tap-clap, tap-clap, tap-clap, tap-clap
toes   toes   toes   toes

Ev'ry Time I Feel the Spirit

Black Spiritual

A REFRAIN

Ev - 'ry time I _____ feel the spir - it _____ mov - in'

in my heart ___ I will pray; Ev - 'ry time I _____ feel the

spir - it _____ mov - in' in my heart ___ I will pray.

B

1. Up on the moun - tain _____ when my Lord spoke,
2. I got a home in _____ the Prom - ised Land,

18

Out   of   His   mouth   came ____ fire   and   smoke,
Ain't gon - na   stop   till   I   shake   His   hand,

I   looked a - round   me, ____ It   looked   so   fine,
Now Jor - dan   riv - er ____ is   chilly   and   cold,

D.C. al Fine

I   asked   my   Lord   if ____ all   was   mine.
It   chills   the   bod - y ____ not   the   soul.

Bell Part for Section A

Percussion Parts for Section A

Which part will you play to accompany section A of "Ev'ry Time I Feel the Spirit"?

Drum $\frac{4}{4}$

Tambourine $\frac{4}{4}$

Triangle $\frac{4}{4}$

A Solo-Chorus Song

Keep time to the music of this lively spiritual by tapping
your foot during section A and snapping your fingers
during section B.

Keep in the Middle of the Road

Black Spiritual

1. I hear them an-gels call-in' loud, Keep in the mid-dle of the road, They are wait-in' there in a great big crowd, Keep in the mid-dle of the road, I can see them stand-in''round the big white gate, Gon-na trav-el a-long_ be-fore it gets too late, For it ain't no use for to sit down, and wait, Keep in the mid-dle of the road. _____

So chil-dren keep in the mid-dle of the road, Chil-dren keep in the

mid-dle of the road, Don't you look to the right, don't you look to the left, Just

keep in the mid-dle of the road.

2. I have no time to stop an' talk,
   Keep in the middle of the road,
   'Cause the road is rough an' it's hard to walk,
   Keep in the middle of the road.
   Gonna fix my eyes on the golden stair,
   Gonna keep on a-goin' 'til I get there,
   For my head is bound that crown for to wear,
   Keep in the middle of the road. (Refrain)

3. The world is full of sinful things,
   Keep in the middle of the road,
   When your feet get tired put on your wings,
   Keep in the middle of the road.
   When you lay down in that road to die,
   Watch them angels in the sky,
   Put on your wings and get up an' fly,
   Keep in the middle of the road. (Refrain)

Here is a tambourine pattern to play on the chorus parts
in section A of the song.

(Shake   hit   hit)

Make up your own tambourine pattern to play during
section B.

A Song in Gospel Style

Edith Wharton, a famous American novelist, wrote:

"There are two ways of spreading light; to be the candle or the mirror that reflects it."

What do you think the author meant?

You can sing about your "little light" in this joyful gospel song.

This Little Light of Mine

Black Spiritual

This lit-tle light of mine, I'm gon-na let it shine,

This lit-tle light of mine, I'm gon-na let it shine,

This lit-tle light of mine, I'm gon-na let it shine,

Let it shine, let it shine, let it shine.____

On Mon-day he gave me the gift___ of love, _ on Tues-day peace came

from a - bove, _ on Wednes-day he told me to have _ more faith, _ on

Thurs-day he gave me just a lit-tle more grace. _ On Fri-day he told me to watch_

_ and pray, _ on Sat-ur-day told me just what to say, _ on

Sun-day gave me the gift di-vine _ just to let my lit-tle light shine.

Patterns for Tambourine

You can use these patterns to accompany section A of the song. Which pattern will you try first?

(This   lit - tle light of)

A Sunrise Call

Songs and dances are of great importance in the
ceremonies and rituals of Native Americans. Here is a song
that the Zuni Indians sing in a ceremony to greet the sun.

As you listen to the song, play a steady-beat drum pattern
on your desk.

Zuni Sunrise Song

Zuni Indian Song   Translation by Carlos Troyer

Rise! _____ A - rise! _____ A - rise!

Rise! _____ A - rise! _____ A - rise!

Wake ye, a - rise! Life is greet - ing thee.

Wake ye, a - rise! Ev - er watch - ful be.

Moth - er God of Life, She is call - ing thee!

Moth - er   God   of   Life,   She   is   greet - ing   thee!

f

Rise! _____   A - rise! _____   A - rise!

p *(Echo)*

Rise! _____   A - rise! _____   A - rise!

In this poem, Indians of the Navajo tribe
express their love of beauty
in the world around them.

House Made of Dawn

House made of dawn
House made of evening light,
House made of dark cloud . . .
Dark cloud is at the house's door,
The trail out of it is dark cloud,
The zigzag lightening stands high upon it . . .
Happily may I walk.
Happily, with abundant showers, may I walk.
Happily, with abundant plants, may I walk.
Happily, on the trail of pollen, may I walk.
Happily may I walk.
May it be beautiful before me.
May it be beautiful behind me.
May it be beautiful below me.
May it be beautiful above me.
May it be beautiful all around me.
In beauty it is finished.

From Patterns and Ceremonials of Indians of the Southwest

A Song of the American Revolution

"Yankee Doodle" is the most famous song to come out of the American Revolution. But "Johnny Has Gone for a Soldier" is probably the most beautiful.

As you listen to the recording, imagine the sadness felt by a young woman when someone she loved went to fight in the war.

Johnny Has Gone for a Soldier

Song of the American Revolution   Collected by John Allison

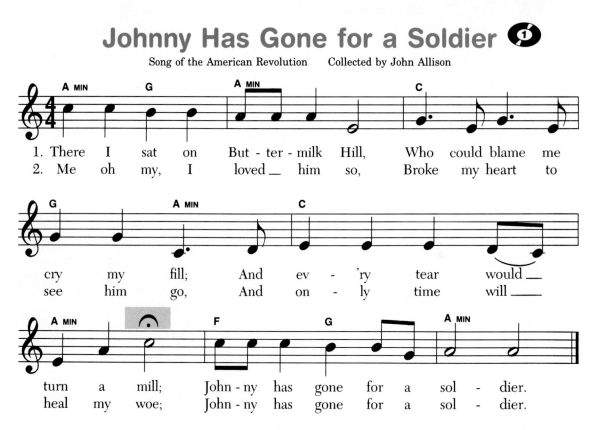

1. There I sat on But-ter-milk Hill, Who could blame me
2. Me oh my, I loved him so, Broke my heart to

cry my fill; And ev-'ry tear would
see him go, And on-ly time will

turn a mill; John-ny has gone for a sol - dier.
heal my woe; John-ny has gone for a sol - dier.

3. I'll sell my flax, I'll sell my wheel,
Buy my love a sword of steel
So it in battle he may wield;
Johnny has gone for a soldier.

Washington

He played by the river when he was young,
He raced with rabbits along the hills,
He fished for minnows, and climbed and swung,
And hooted back at the whippoorwills.
Strong and slender and tall he grew—
And then, one morning, the bugles blew.

Over the hills the summons came,
Over the river's shining rim.
He said that the bugles called his name,
He knew that his country needed him,
And he answered, "Coming!" and marched away
For many a night and many a day.

Perhaps when the marches were hot and long
He'd think of the river flowing by
Or, camping under the winter sky,
Would hear the whippoorwill's far-off song.
Boy or soldier, in peace or strife,
He loved America all his life!

Nancy Byrd Turner

The following resolution was presented to the House of Representatives on the death of our first President.

To the memory of the Man, first in war, first in peace, and first in the hearts of his countrymen.

A Concerto by Haydn

A concerto is a composition written for solo instrument with orchestra. You will hear the last movement of a concerto by Franz Joseph Haydn. What solo instrument do you hear in this piece? Listen for the parts where the solo instrument plays alone and where the orchestra plays alone.

   Concerto in D Major, Movement 3 .... Haydn

This little folk-dance tune is heard many times throughout the piece. Sometimes it is played by the piano, and at other times, by the orchestra.

Listen for the short notes that decorate the music. These short notes are called *grace notes*.

Here are two other themes to listen for.

Haydn was born in a small village in Austria. His father made wheels for carriages, and his mother was a cook in the household of a count. When Haydn was a little boy, he would pretend to play the violin with two pieces of wood as he listened to his mother singing the folk songs of the area. It is possible that one of the songs she sang was the little dance tune Haydn used in his *Concerto in D Major*.

In 1761 a wealthy Austrian nobleman named Esterhazy hired Haydn to write music for his private orchestra. In those days, every castle had its own band of professional musicians. For 30 years, Haydn lived at the Esterhazy castle. Although a musician living in a nobleman's house was nothing more than a servant, Haydn never minded. He was a simple man who was grateful for the opportunity to compose and perform music.

Franz Joseph Haydn
(1732–1809)

29

A Fife and Drum Tune

The melody of this song is a favorite with fife and drum corps. It has been used as a parade tune for many years. Try drumming a steady-beat pattern on your knees as you listen to the music.

The Girl I Left Behind Me

Irish Folk Song

1. I'm ___ lone - some since I crossed the hill,
2. My ___ mind her beau - ty will re - tain,

And o'er the moor ___ and ___ val - ley
In sleep - ing or ___ in ___ wak - ing

Such ___ heav - y thoughts my heart do fill
Un - til I see my love a - gain;

Since part - ing with my ___ Sal - ly.
For her my heart is ___ ach - ing.

I ___ seek no more the fine and gay
But ___ now I'm off for Brigh - ton Camp

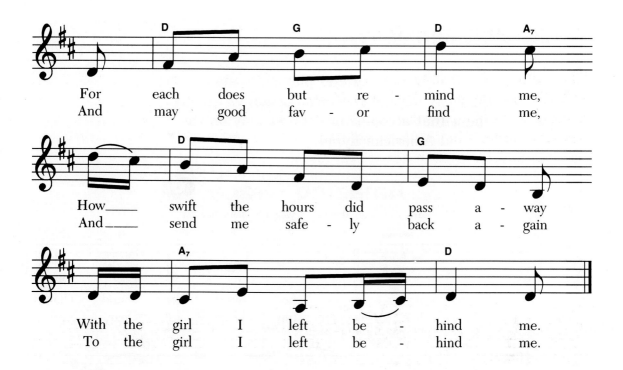

For each does but re - mind me,
And may good fav - or find me,

How____ swift the hours did pass a - way
And____ send me safe - ly back a - gain

With the girl I left be - hind me.
To the girl I left be - hind me.

Cowboy Version

This Irish song found its way to America when our country
was very young. Later on it traveled westward with the
pioneers and became a cowboy favorite. Here are the
words that the cowhands sang.

1. I struck the trail in seventy-nine,
   The herd strung out behind me;
   As I jogged along, my mind ran back
   To the gal I left behind me.
   If ever I get off the trail
   And the rustlers they don't find me,
   I'll make my way straight back again
   To the gal I left behind me.

2. When the night was dark and the cattle run,
   With the boys comin' on behind me,
   As I followed the track my mind ran back
   To the gal I left behind me.
   The wind did blow, the rain did flow,
   The hail did fall and blind me;
   I thought of that gal, that sweet little gal,
   That gal I left behind me.

Here is the cowboy version of "The Girl I Left Behind Me."
Follow the words as you listen to the recording. You might
try singing along.

The Girl I Left Behind Me .... Cowboy Version

31

An Early American Hymn

"Amazing Grace" has been sung and played by many people since the early days of America. Listen especially for the instrument that accompanies the melody on the recording of this old American hymn.

Amazing Grace

Early American Melody   Words by John Newton

1. A - maz - ing ___ grace, how sweet the sound, That
2. 'Twas grace that ___ taught my heart to fear, And

saved a ___ wretch like me! ___ I once ___ was ___
grace my ___ fears re - lieved; ___ How pre - cious ___

lost, but now ___ am ___ found, Was blind, but ___
did that grace ___ ap - pear The hour I ___

now I see. ___
first be - lieved! ___

3. Through many dangers, toils, and snares,
   I have already come;
   'Tis grace has brought me safe thus far,
   And grace will lead me home.

4. The Lord has promised good to me,
   His word my hope secures;
   He will my shield and portion be
   As long as life endures.

Listen to another performance of "Amazing Grace." This version might be heard in some churches today. How is it different from the first recording you heard?

Amazing Grace, Version 2 . . . . Early American
Melody

Singing Schools

If you had been an early settler in the South, you might have attended a *singing school.* You would have used music that was written in a strange-looking notation called *shaped notes.* Each notehead represented a syllable.

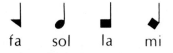

fa   sol   la   mi

Here is what the music of "Amazing Grace" looked like in those singing-school days.

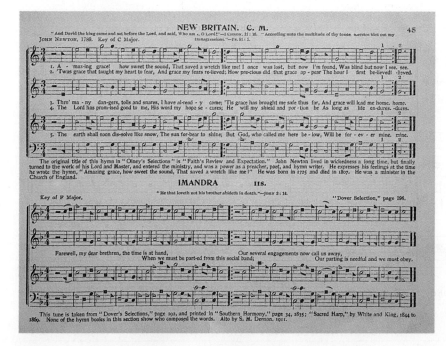

Here is what the music sounded like in those singing-school days.

Amazing Grace, Version 3 . . . . Early American
Melody

Across the Wide Prairies

Imagine what it must have been like to travel across the country in a covered wagon in the year 1849. You would have needed more than just a sense of humor to do it!

Sweet Betsy from Pike

American Folk Song

REFRAIN

B Too - ra - lee,_____ too - ra - lay,_____

F C

Too - ra - lee, too - ra - lay,

C   G₇   C

Sing-ing too - ra - lee, too - ra - lee, too - ra - lee ay.

3. They soon reached the desert where Betsy gave out,
   And down on the sand she lay rolling about.
   While Ike, in great tears, looked on in surprise:
   Said, "Betsy, get up, you'll get sand in your eyes." *Refrain*

4. The rooster ran off and the oxen all died;
   The last piece of bacon that morning was fried.
   Poor Ike got discouraged and Betsy got mad;
   The dog wagged his tail and looked awfully sad. *Refrain*

5. The alkali desert was burning and hot,
   And Ike, he decided to leave on the spot:
   "My dear old Pike County, I'll go back to you."
   Said Betsy, "You'll go by yourself if you do." *Refrain*

6. They swam the wide rivers, they crossed the tall peaks,
   They camped out on prairies for weeks and for weeks,
   Fought hunger and rattlers and big storms of dust,
   Determined to reach California or bust. *Refrain*

New Words for Old Tunes

People are always adding new words to old folk tunes. Can
you think of a new verse to add to this old story of Betsy
and Ike?

A Song from American History

This song is probably the best-known song from the Civil War period. To feel its marching beat, chant the following pattern softly as you listen to the music.

March - ing,   march - ing

When Johnny Comes Marching Home

Words and Music by Patrick S. Gilmore

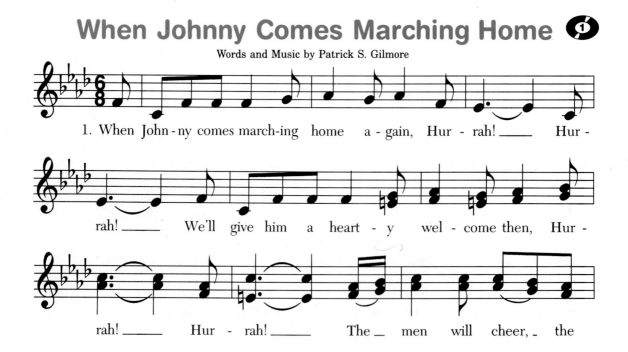

1. When John - ny comes march - ing home a - gain, Hur - rah! _____ Hur -

rah! _____ We'll give him a heart - y wel - come then, Hur -

rah! _____ Hur - rah! _____ The _ men will cheer, _ the

boys will shout, The la - dies they _ will all turn out, And we'll

shout, "Hur - rah" when John - ny comes march - ing home. _

2. Let love and friendship on the day, Hurrah! Hurrah!
   Their choicest treasure then display, Hurrah! Hurrah!
   And let each one perform some part,
   To fill with joy the warrior's heart,
   And we'll shout, "Hurrah" when Johnny comes marching home!

3. Get ready for the jubilee, Hurrah! Hurrah!
   We'll give the hero three times three, Hurrah! Hurrah!
   The laurel wreath is ready now
   To place upon his royal brow,
   And we'll shout, "Hurrah" when Johnny comes marching home!

Chant and Play

Use one of these patterns to accompany the song.
Will you chant the pattern, or will you play it on
a percussion instrument?

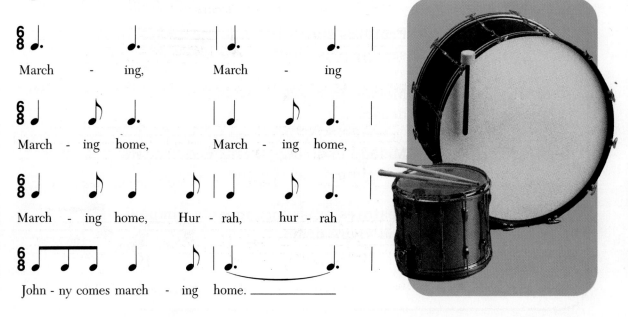

March - ing, March - ing

March - ing home, March - ing home,

March - ing home, Hur - rah, hur - rah

John - ny comes march - ing home. _____

37

You will hear a familiar tune in this piece. Following the chart will help you hear what is going on as the music goes along.

 American Salute .... Gould

1 INTRODUCTION: Full orchestra; "Johnny comes marching home" rhythm (♪♪♪♪ ♩ ♪ ♩.); snare drum solo

2 MAIN THEME: Melody in bassoons accompanied by snare drum and violins; harp plays downward-moving pattern toward the end

3 INTERLUDE: Features snare drum; brass and strings play "hurrah" figures (♪ ♩.)

4 MAIN THEME: Melody in woodwinds; bell tones decorate

5 MAIN THEME: Melody in strings; brass instruments and timpani at the end

6 INTERLUDE: Features brass instruments, timpani, and snare drum

7 VARIATION 1: Bustling tune played softly by woodwinds, accompanied by harps and plucked strings; ends with rising scale passage

8 INTERLUDE: Whirling figure in strings

9 VARIATION 2: Melody played by full orchestra with brass and percussion highlighted; faster tempo; loud and jazzy

10 INTERLUDE: Strings, French horns, and bassoons play downward-moving chords; chimes and snare drum

11 VARIATION 3: Melody played slowly by trumpets and trombones over marching chord pattern; gets softer and softer; ends with little jigging tune, first in woodwinds, then in trumpets and trombones

12 INTERLUDE: Musical conversation between woodwinds and strings, then French horns and trombones

13 MAIN THEME: Introduced by timpani and snare drum; melody in woodwinds and strings, getting faster and louder to the end

14 CODA: Features timpani and snare drum; woodwinds and brass added gradually; main theme played by full orchestra; ends with "Johnny comes marching home" rhythm

Casey at the Throttle

Casey Jones was known for the speed at which he could
make a train travel and for the wonderful sound he could
get out of the train whistle. Some stories tell us that the
people who worked in the fields near the railroad track
could tell when Casey was at the throttle by the sound of
the train whistle.

Casey Jones

Words by T. Lawrence Seibert   Music by Eddie Newton

1. Come, all you round-ers, if you want __ to hear
   A sto-ry a-bout __ a __ brave en-gi-neer,
   And Ca-sey Jones __ was the round-er's name,
   On a six eight wheel-er boys, he won __ his fame.
   The cal-ler called Ca-sey at a half __ past four.

2. Put in your wa-ter and __ shov-el your coal,
   Put your head out the win-dow, watch them driv-ers roll,
   I'll run her till __ she __ leaves __ the rail,
   'Cause I'm eight hours late __ with that West-ern mail.
   He looked at his watch __ and his watch __ was slow,

3. Ca-sey pulled up __ at __ Re-no hill,
   He too-ted for the cross-ing with an aw-ful shrill,
   The switch-man knew __ by the en-gine's moan
   That the man at the throt-tle was __ Ca-sey Jones.
   He pulled up with-in __ two __ miles of the place,

Ca - sey kissed his ____ wife ___ at the sta - tion door,
He ___ looked at the wa - ter and the wa - ter was low,
And ___ Num - ber ____ Four ___ stared him in ___ the face,

He mount - ed to the cab - in with his or - ders in his hand,
He turned ___ to the fire - man and then ___ he ___ said,
He turned ___ to the fire - man, said, "Boy, you bet - ter jump,

And he took his fare - well trip ___ to the Prom - ised Land.
"We're ___ goin' to reach ___ Fris - co, but we'll all ___ be dead."
'Cause there's two ___ lo - co - mo - tives that's a - go - in' to bump."

REFRAIN

Ca - sey Jones, ___
{ Mount - ed to the cab - in,
{ Goin' to reach ___ Fris - co,
{ Two ___ lo - co - mo - tives,

Ca - sey Jones, ___
{ With his or - ders in his hands,
{ But we'll all ___ be ___ dead,
{ That's a - go - in' to bump,

Ca - sey Jones, ___
{ Mount - ed to the cab - in,
{ Goin' to reach ___ Fris - co,
{ Two ___ lo - co - mo - tives,

And he took his fare - well trip ___ to the Prom - ised Land.
We're ___ goin' to reach ___ Fris - co, but we'll all ___ be dead.
There's ___ two ___ lo - co - mo - tives that's a - go - in' to bump.

41

Song of a Great River

One of the verses in this song about the great Columbia River mentions six other rivers of the Northwest. What are their names? Can you find them on a map?

Roll On, Columbia

Words by Woody Guthrie
Music Based on "Goodnight, Irene" by Huddie Ledbetter and John Lomax

1. Green Doug - las fir where the wa - ters cut through,
2. Oth - er big riv-ers add ___ pow - er to you,

Down her wild moun - tains and can - yons she flew Ca -
Yak - i - ma, Snake, and the Klick - i - tat, too. ___

na - di - an North-west to the o - cean so blue,
Sand - y, Wil - lam - ette, and the Hood Riv - er, too,

Roll on Co - lum - bia, roll on. ___
Roll on Co - lum - bia, roll on. ___

REFRAIN

Countermelody

Roll - ing a - long, Roll - ing a - long, Roll - ing a -

F   **C₇**

Roll on, _____ Co - lum - bia, roll on, Roll

long, _____ Co - lum - bia, roll on. Your pow - er is turn - ing our

C₇   **F**

on, _____ Co - lum - bia, roll on. Your pow - er is turn - ing our

dark - ness to dawn, Roll on, Co - lum - bia, roll on, roll on.

B♭   **C₇**   **F**

dark - ness to dawn, Roll on, Co - lum - bia, roll on. _____

3. At Bonneville now there are ships in the locks,
   The water has risen and covered the rocks,
   Shiploads a-plenty are soon past the docks,
   Roll on, Columbia, roll on. *Refrain*

4. And on up the river is the Grand Coulee Dam,
   The biggest thing built by the hand of a man,
   To run the great fact'ries and water the land,
   Roll on, Columbia, roll on. *Refrain*

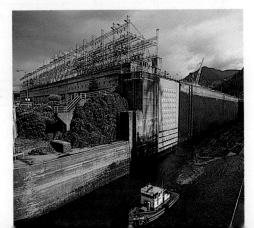

In Praise of Friendship

What could be more important
than having loyal friends!
What important things can one
good friend offer to another?
Pete Seeger offers this song as
a gift to his friends everywhere.

Do a tap-snap pattern as you
listen to this song. Try this one,
then make up your own pattern.

(tap snap tap snap)

Precious Friends

Words and Music by Pete Seeger

Just when I thought — all was lost — you changed my mind. —

You gave me hope, not just the old soft soap, You showed that

we could learn to share in time, You and I and ev-'ry-bod - y,

I'll keep plug-gin' — on, — Your face will shine — so sweet and

Folk Songs of Tomorrow

The songs that folksingers make up today are recorded and are played on radio and television, so that people all over the world hear and sing each other's tunes. Those that you will remember and sing often will be the folk songs of tomorrow.

In this recording you will hear a popular recording group singing a special arrangement of Stephen Foster's hit song "Oh, Susanna."

LISTENING SKILLS 2   Oh, Susanna . . . . Stephen Foster

An Instant Hit

Stephen Foster (1826–1864) composed
songs that are still popular with people
everywhere. In fact, some of Foster's
songs have become so well known that
they are often referred to as American
folk songs.

When "Nelly Bly" was published
in February 1850, it became an instant
hit. Because of its lively melody and
humorous words, this song has been
a favorite ever since.

Nelly Bly

Words and Music by Stephen C. Foster

1. Nel - ly Bly! Nel - ly Bly! Bring the broom a - long.
2. Nel - ly Bly! has a voice Like a tur - tle dove,

We'll sweep the kitch - en clean, my dear, And have a lit - tle song
I hear it in the mead - ow and I hear it in the grove.

Poke the wood, my la - dy love, And make the fire __ burn,
Nel - ly Bly __ has a heart __ warm as a cup of tea,

And while I take the ban - jo down, Just give the mush a turn.
And big - ger than the sweet po - ta - to Down in Ten - nes - see.

REFRAIN

Hey, Nel-ly! Ho, Nel-ly! Lis-ten, love, to me;

I'll sing for you, play for you a dul-cem mel-o-dy.

Hey, Nel-ly! Ho, Nel-ly! Lis-ten, love, to me;

I'll sing for you, play for you a dul-cem mel-o-dy.

3. Nelly Bly! Nelly Bly! Never, never sigh,
    Never bring a teardrop to the corner of your eye.
    For the pie is made of pumpkins and the mush is made of corn,
    And there's corn and pumpkins plenty, love, A-lying in the barn. *(Refrain)*

Close Harmony

This song has two sections—A and B. In which section do you see a harmony part written?

Listen to the recording and check your answer.

The Sidewalks of New York

Music by James W. Blake   Words by Charles B. Lawlor

Down in front of Ca - sey's, ___ Old brown wood - en

stoop, ___ On a sum - mer's eve - ning ___ we

An Old Favorite

This song is still high on the list of favorites at parties
when people gather around the piano to sing. Sing along
when you can.

In the Good Old Summer Time

George Evans

In the good old sum - mer time, sum - mer time, In the

good old sum - mer time, _____ Stroll - ing through the

shad - y lanes stroll - ing with your ba - by

mine, ba - by mine, You hold her hand and she holds

yours, And that's a ver - y good sign, a good sign That

she's your toot - sey woot - sey in the good old sum - mer time. _____

54

Add Triangle and Drum

These percussion parts may be used to accompany "In the Good Old Summer Time." Choose a partner and practice the parts together.

Triangle $\frac{3}{4}$ 𝅗𝅥. | 𝅗𝅥. | 𝅗𝅥. | 𝅗𝅥. |

Low drum $\frac{3}{4}$ 𝄽 ♩ ♩ | 𝄽 ♩ ♩ | 𝄽 ♩ ♩ | 𝄽 ♩ ♩ |

Summer Concert in the Park

Band concerts in the park have been a favorite pastime of the American people for years. If you had lived in New York City during the middle of the twentieth century, you might have gone to a summer-evening concert in New York's Central Park. Here is one of the band pieces you might have heard.

Semper Fidelis . . . . Sousa

From Old Broadway

George M. Cohan is an important figure in the history of the American musical theater. Cohan not only wrote the music and the words for his songs, but he also wrote the plays in which they were sung.

Cohan produced his first full-length Broadway success in 1904. It was called *Little Johnny Jones,* and it contained two of his best-known songs—"Yankee Doodle Boy" and "Give My Regards to Broadway."

Give My Regards to Broadway

Words and Music by George M. Cohan

Give my re-gards to Broad - way, Re - mem-ber me to

Give my re-gards to Broad - way, Re - mem-ber me to

Her - ald Square, oh, go on and Tell all the gang at For - ty -

Her - ald Square, _____ Tell all the gang at For - ty -

se-cond Street that I will soon be there; oh, go on and

se-cond Street that I will soon be there; _____

Whis-per of how I'm yearn - ing To min-gle with the

Whis-per of how I'm yearn - ing To min-gle with the

old time throng, oh, go on and Give my re - gards to old Broad -

old - time throng, _____ Give my re - gards to old Broad -

way, And say that I'll be there ere long. _____

way, And say that I'll be there ere long. _____

Singing Across the Country

This song was inspired by a cross-country trip made in two Oldsmobiles. It took 44 days to make the trip from Detroit, Michigan, to Portland, Oregon. How long do you think it would take a modern car to make the same trip today?

In My Merry Oldsmobile

Music by Gus Edwards   Words by Vincent Bryan

Come a - way with me Lu - cille _____ In my

mer - ry Olds - mo - bile, _____ Down the road of

life we'll fly Au - to - mo - bub - bling you and I.

To the church we'll swift - ly steal _____ Then our

58

wed - ding bells will peal _____ You can go as far as you

like with me In my mer - ry Olds - mo - bile. _____

Name-That-Tune Challenge

Here are the beginnings of three American songs that were
written between 1894 and 1905. The notation shows only
the rhythm of the words (the melodic rhythm). Can you
name each song?

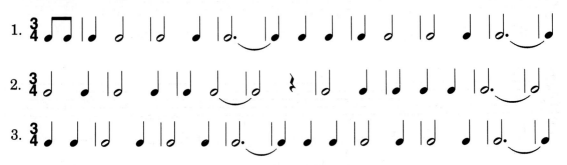

Ev'rybody Rock

You'll be able to join in on the last four lines of this rock 'n roll song the first time you hear it:

Rock and Roll Is Here to Stay

Words and Music by David White

1. Rock and roll is here to stay, and it will nev-er die.
2. If you don't like rock and roll, just think what you've been miss-in', But

It was meant to be that way, though I don't know why. ____
if you like to hop and stroll, walk a-round and lis-ten.

I don't care what peo-ple say, Rock and roll is here to stay!
Let's all start to rock and roll, Ev-'ry-bod-y rock and roll.

Chorus

We don't care what peo-ple say, ___ Rock and roll is here to stay. ___

Solo

Rock and roll will al-ways be, I dig it to the end,

It-'ll go down in his-to-ry, Just you watch, my friend.

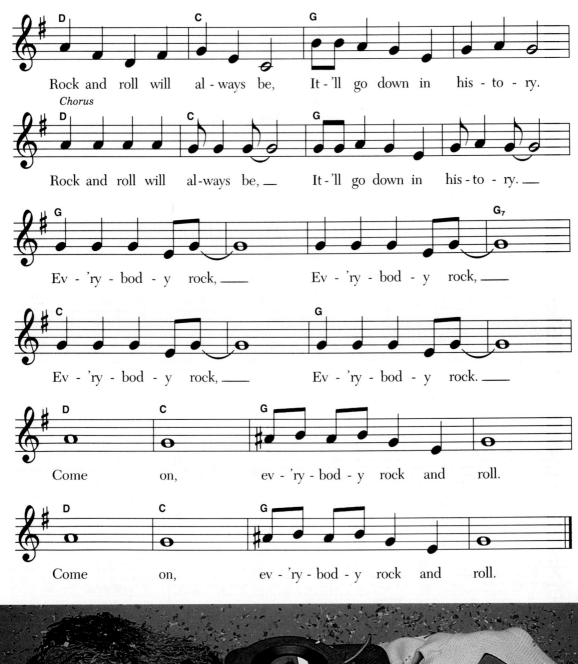

Rock and roll will al-ways be, It-'ll go down in his-to-ry.

Chorus

Rock and roll will al-ways be, — It-'ll go down in his-to-ry. —

Ev-'ry-bod-y rock, — Ev-'ry-bod-y rock, —

Ev-'ry-bod-y rock, — Ev-'ry-bod-y rock. —

Come on, ev-'ry-bod-y rock and roll.

Come on, ev-'ry-bod-y rock and roll.

Pete Seeger—Folksinger and Composer

"Turn, Turn, Turn" was written by Pete Seeger, one of
America's most famous folksingers. Follow the music
as you listen to the recording. Join in on section A
when you can.

Turn, Turn, Turn
(To Everything There Is a Season)

Words from the Book of Ecclesiastes   Adaptation and Music by Pete Seeger

To ev-'ry - thing, (Turn, turn, turn) There is a sea-son (Turn, turn, turn) And a time for ev - 'ry pur-pose un - der heav - en.

1. A time to be born, a time to die; A time to plant, a time to reap; A time to kill, a time to
2. A time to build up, a time to break down; A time to dance, a time to mourn; A time to cast a - way
3. A time of love, a time of hate; A time of war, a time of peace; A time you may em -
4. A time to gain, a time to lose; A time to rend, a time to sew; A time to love, a time to

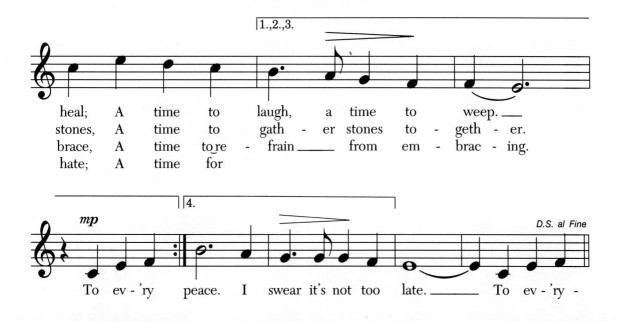

heal; A time to laugh, a time to weep. ___
stones, A time to gath - er stones to - geth - er.
brace, A time to re - frain ___ from em - brac - ing.
hate; A time for

mp

D.S. al Fine

To ev - 'ry peace. I swear it's not too late. ___ To ev - 'ry -

"Precious Friends" is another song by Pete Seeger.
You will find the song and a photograph of the
composer on page 44 in your book.

Added Parts for Section B

Recorder or Bells

A time to be born, a time to die; A time to plant, a time to

Countermelody

Turn, Turn, Turn, Turn, Turn,

reap; A time to kill, a time to heal; A time to laugh, a time to weep.

Turn, Turn, Turn, Turn, Turn, Turn, Turn.

Careers in Music

On this recording, Mike Reid talks about his career in music.

Careers in Music—
Mike Reid

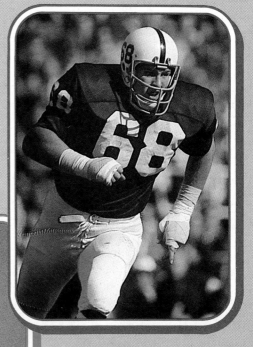

Melody and Countermelody

Listen for the instruments that are featured in the recording of "Johnny's My Boy." To which family of instruments do they belong—string, woodwind, brass, or percussion?

Tap a strong steady drumbeat on your knees as you listen to the song.

Johnny's My Boy

Folk Song from Ghana Countermelodies by Max V. Exner

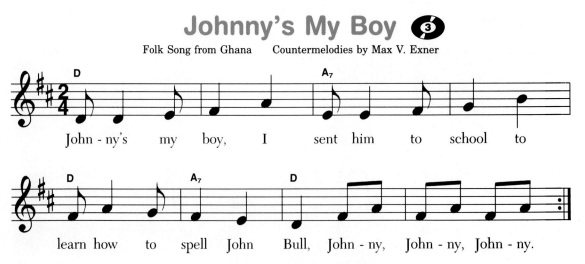

John - ny's   my   boy,   I   sent him   to   school   to

learn how   to   spell   John   Bull,   John - ny,   John - ny, John - ny.

Add a Countermelody

Countermelody 1

John - ny,   John - ny, John - ny, _____ John - ny,   John - ny, John - ny. _____

Countermelody 2

John - ny, _____ John - ny, John - ny, _____ John - ny, _____ John - ny, John - ny. _____

Countermelody Challenge

When you are able to sing the countermelodies notated above, try this one.

Countermelody 3

John - ny's my boy, _____ and I sent him to school _____ for to

learn how to spell _____ John - ny Bull; _____ John - ny!

Drum Patterns

Which drum pattern will you use to accompany "Johnny's My Boy"?

Layers of Sound

There are six different parts in this song. Can you find the signs that tell you to sing each part two times?

On the recording you will hear how the parts (layers of sound) are put together.

Banuwa ③

Folk Song from Liberia

Ba - nu - wa, ba - nu - wa, ba - nu - wa yo. _____

Ba - nu - wa, ba - nu - wa, ba - nu - wa yo. _____

A - la - no, neh - ni a - la - no;

a - la - no, neh - ni a - la - no.

Neh - ni a - la - no; Neh - ni a - la - no.

Neh - ni a - la - no; Neh - ni a - la - no.

Ba - nu - wa, ba - nu - wa, ba - nu - wa yo. _____

After you have listened to this drum music from Africa,
improvise your own drum part as the class sings
"Banuwa."

Drum Music .... **Africa**

The Rhythm of the Sea

This old Northumberland folk song tells about the long and lonely wait for a sailor's return from the sea.

Feel the gentle rocking motion in the music as you listen to this song of the sea.

Blow the Wind Southerly

Northumbrian Folk Song

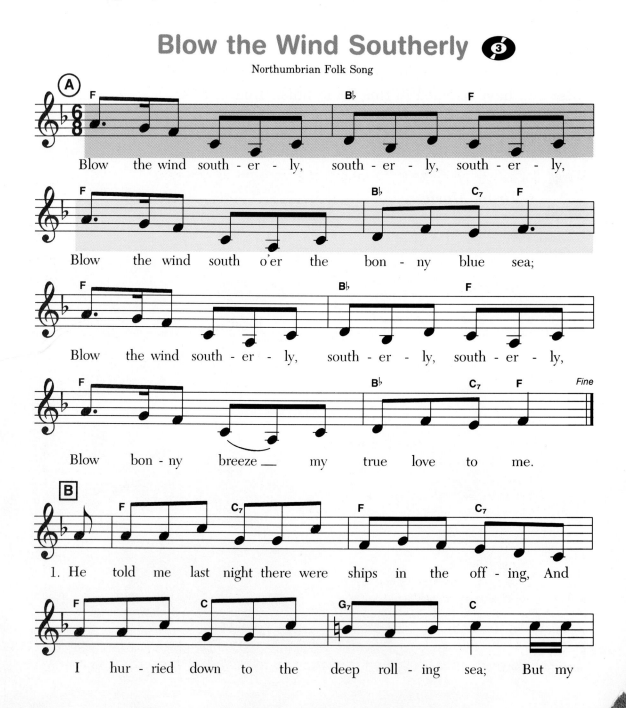

Blow the wind south - er - ly, south - er - ly, south - er - ly,

Blow the wind south o'er the bon - ny blue sea;

Blow the wind south - er - ly, south - er - ly, south - er - ly,

Blow bon - ny breeze — my true love to me.

1. He told me last night there were ships in the off - ing, And

I hur - ried down to the deep roll - ing sea; But my

70

eye could not see it, wher - ev - er might be it, The

bark that is bear - ing my true love to me.

D.C. al Fine

2. I stood by the lighthouse that last time we parted,
   Till darkness came down o'er the deep rolling sea;
   And no longer I saw the bright bark of my true love.
   Blow bonny breeze and bring him to me.

What does this poem tell you about the rhythm of the sea?

Long Trip

The sea is a wilderness of waves,
A desert of water.
We dip and dive,
Rise and roll,
Hide and are hidden
On the sea,
   Day, night,
   Night, day,
The sea is a desert of waves,
A wilderness of water.

Langston Hughes

A Folk Song from Mexico

When you listen to the recording of this song, you will hear the voices singing in two parts. How are the parts alike? How are they different? Following the score will help you answer the questions.

Laredo

Mexican Folk Song   English Words by Margaret Marks

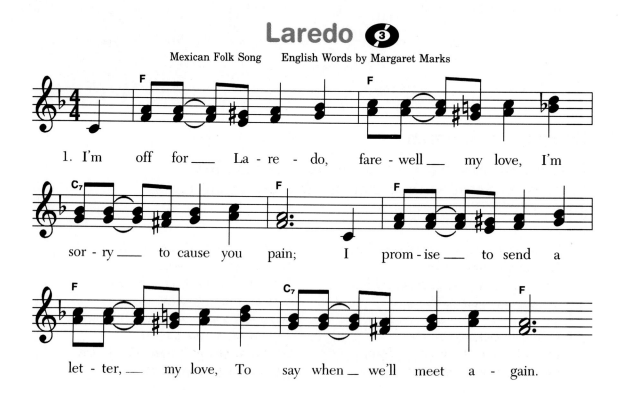

1. I'm off for Laredo, farewell my love, I'm sorry to cause you pain; I promise to send a letter, my love, To say when we'll meet again.

Don't fol-low — a-cross the prai-rie, — my love, Don't fol-low — me where I go, But wait till — I send a mes-sage, — my love, Till then I — will miss you so.

2. I've brought you a hand-sewn saddle, my love,
   A blanket and bridle fine;
   So when you go past the bunkhouse, my love,
   The cowboys will know you're mine.
   I've brought you a key of silver, my love,
   Attached to a golden chain,
   To lock up your heart forever, my love,
   If never we meet again.

Singing in Spanish

Here are the Spanish words of "Laredo." Try to follow
them as you listen to the recording. You might want to try
singing along.

1. *Ya me voy, para el Laredo, mi bien*
   Te vengo á decir adiós.
   Ya me voy, para el Laredo, mi bien
   Te vengo á decir adiós.
   De allá te mando decir, mi bien,
   Como se mancuernan dos.
   De allá te mando decir, mi bien,
   Como se mancuernan dos.

2. *Toma esa llavita de oro, mi bien,*
   Abre mi pecho y verás:
   Toma esa llavita de oro, mi bien,
   Abre mi pecho y verás:
   Lo mucho que yo te quiero, mi bien,
   Y el mal pago que me dás.
   Lo mucho que yo te quiero, mi bien,
   Y el mal pago que me dás.

A Mexican-American Favorite

"De Colores" tells about the beauty that can be found in the simple things of life—fields in spring colors; brightly colored birds that come from far-away places; a rainbow that splashes its colors across the sky.

Follow the melody line as you listen to the song. Sing along when you can.

De Colores

Traditional   English Words by Alice Firgau

When ___ the mead - ows, ___ when the mead - ows burst forth in the
De ___ co - lo - res, ___ De co - lo - res se vis - ten los

cool dew - y col - ors of spring - time; ___
cam - pos en la pri - ma - ve - ra, ___

When ___ the swal - lows, ___ when the swal - lows come wing - ing in
De ___ co - lo - res, ___ De co - lo - res son los pa - ja -

clouds of bright col - ors from far - off; ___
ri - tos que vie - nen dea - fue - ra, ___

When ___ the rain - bow, ___ when the rain - bow spreads rib - bons of
De ___ co - lo - res, ___ De co - lo - res es el ar - co

74

col - or   all   o - ver   the   sky: _____   Then   I   know   why   the
i - res   que   ve - mos   lu - cir, _____   y   por   e - so   los

splen - dors   of   true   love   are   great   and   their   col - ors,   the
gran - des   a - mo - res   de   mu - chos   co - lo - res   me

1.
best ones   of   all. _____
gus - tan   a   mí. _____

2.
best ones   of   all. _____
gus - tan   a   mí. _____

A Pueblo Indian girl gives her definition of beauty in this
poem.

BEAUTY

Beauty is seen
In the sunlight,
The trees, the birds,
Corn growing and people working
Or dancing for their harvest.

Beauty is heard
In the night,
Wind sighing, rain falling,
Or a singer chanting
Anything in earnest.

Beauty is in yourself.
Good deeds, happy thoughts
That repeat themselves
In your dreams,
In your work,
And even in your rest.

E-Yeh-Shure'

75

Folk Song from China

To people from China, as to people from all over the world, a new moon is an object of great beauty. It is also a symbol of new hopes for a better life.

The lyrics of "Crescent Moon" paint a word picture. Read the three verses of the song as you would a poem. Try to picture in your mind the scenes that the words suggest.

Crescent Moon

English Words by Elaine Nienow   Chinese Folk Song

1. Cres - cent moon float - ing on a cloud   O'er the crest of the
2. Night - in - gale sing - ing in the wood,   Ser - e - nad - ing the
3. Lo - tus blooms rise a - bove the streams,   Love - ly wax - en per -

moun - tain.   Sil - ver gem in a sat - in crown,
for - est,   Fills the air with a sad re - frain
fec - tion,   Slow - ly o - pen to view the world,

Rest - ing on the roy - al moun - tain.   Pale moon, new moon,
In the qui - et of the eve - ning.   Sweet song, fair song,
Slow - ly spread their silk - en pet - als.   Wild flow'r, pink flow'r,

1.,2.   3.

cres - cent moon _   Shin - ing bright - ly o - ver K'an - ting.
lone - ly song _   Ech - o - ing through all of K'an - ting.
fleet - ing flow'r _   Grow - ing in the stream of   K'an - ting.

Play an Accompaniment

Accompany the song on the autoharp. Press both the D_7 and the D minor buttons at the same time. This will cause the felt dampers to silence all the strings except the D's and A's. Strum on the first beat of each measure.

You can play this bell ostinato all through the song.

In a Retreat Among Bamboos

Leaning alone in the close bamboos,
I am playing my lute and humming a song
Too softly for anyone to hear—
Except my comrade, the bright moon.

Wang Wei

A Folk Song from Puerto Rico

This Puerto Rican song tells about a bird who is sad and lonely. As he wanders from place to place, the bird sings so no one will know how unhappy he is.

What is the wandering bird searching for?

The Wandering Bird
(El Pájaro Errante)

Puerto Rican

I am a lone - ly wan - der - er, Al - ways lost, I go
Soy pa - ja - ri - llo er-ran - te que an - da per - di - do, que an-

soar - ing all a - lone. I fly to tall cool trees, tall and
da per - di - do, y va por la en - ra - ma - da en

leaf - y trees, search - ing for a home. _____
pos de a - bri - go, en pos de a - bri - go. _____

Al - ways leav - ing, _____ but al-ways sing - ing, _____ They who lis - ten
Al - zo el vue - lo, _____ siem - pre can - tan - do, _____ y el que es-cu-cha no

do not know _____ that I am weep - ing; _____
sa - be ¡Ay! _____ que es - toy llo - ran - do; _____

Al - ways leav - ing, _____ but al-ways sing - ing, _____ They who lis - ten
Al - zo el vue - lo, _____ siem - pre can - tan - do, _____ y el que es-cu-cha no

do not know _____ that I am weep - ing. _____
sa - be ¡Ay! _____ que es - toy llo - ran - do. _____

Three Patterns for Percussion

You can use one of these patterns to accompany "The Wandering Bird." Which pattern will you choose? Play it all through the song.

A Folk Song from Canada

This song comes from our country's neighbor to the north.
The words describe the natural beauty of certain regions of
that vast land. Follow the words as you listen to the song.

Land of the Silver Birch

Folk Song from Canada

1. Land of the sil - ver birch, home of the bea - ver,

Where still the might - y moose wan - ders at will,

Blue lake and rock - y shore, I will re - turn once more.

From collection of Edith Fowke.

REFRAIN

mp D MIN

Boom de de boom boom, Boom de de boom boom, Boom de de boom boom

p _____ *dim.* _____ *pp*

D MIN

Boom. _____

2. Down in the forest, deep in the lowlands,
   My heart cries out for thee, hills of the north.
   Blue lake and rocky shore,
   I will return once more. *(Refrain)*

3. High on a rocky ledge I'll build my wigwam,
   Close by the water's edge, silent and still.
   Blue lake and rocky shore,
   I will return once more. *(Refrain)*

Scored for Percussion

After you have practiced these percussion parts, decide
which pattern you will play as an accompaniment for
"Land of the Silver Birch."

Finland's Celebrated Composer

The Art Museum of Ateneum, Helsinki, Finland

LANDSCAPE 1872
FANNY CHURBERG

Jean Sibelius was not only Finland's most celebrated composer, but he was also an ardent patriot. Much of his music was inspired by the history and legends of his country. Sibelius' *Karelia Suite* was composed to accompany a series of tableaux, each one representing an important moment in the history of Karelia, a province of Finland.

In this recording you will hear a movement from *Karelia Suite*— a movement that Sibelius labeled "Alla Marcia." As you listen to the music, think of what "Alla Marcia" might mean.

"Alla Marcia" from *Karelia Suite* . . . . Sibelius

Sibelius used two main themes in "Alla Marcia." The violins introduce Theme 1 at the very beginning of the piece. How do the tones move in this melody?

Theme 1

Theme 2 sounds a little like a fanfare. You will hear it played first by the trumpets and clarinet, then by the trombones and tuba.

Theme 2

Jean Sibelius
(1865–1957)

Jean Sibelius was born during the last year of Abraham Lincoln's term as president of the United States. Sibelius grew up in a musical atmosphere—there was always music in his home, and the family often went to concerts. Young Janne (as he was called) began taking piano lessons when he was nine years old, but his real interest was making up tunes of his own.

When Sibelius was a young man, he joined the Young Finns, a patriotic group whose purpose was to make the people of Finland more aware of the Finnish arts and culture. It was at this time that Sibelius wrote *Kullervo*, a composition inspired by a great Finnish poem called *Kalevala*, meaning "Land of the Heroes." *Kullervo* was the first of a series of patriotic works that not only made the Finnish people aware of their national heritage but also made Sibelius a national hero.

You will hear seven sets of pieces. When a number is called, listen to both pieces. If you think the pieces are in the same style, circle the words SAME STYLE. If you think the pieces are in different styles, circle the words DIFFERENT STYLES. Listen, then circle your answers on your worksheet.

1 SAME STYLE   DIFFERENT STYLES

2 SAME STYLE   DIFFERENT STYLES

3 SAME STYLE   DIFFERENT STYLES

4 SAME STYLE   DIFFERENT STYLES

5 SAME STYLE   DIFFERENT STYLES

6 SAME STYLE   DIFFERENT STYLES

7 SAME STYLE   DIFFERENT STYLES

Test 1 ✓

After each number you will find a description of a song in your book. Read the song description. Then, from the song list, choose the song that fits the description and, on your worksheet, write its letter in the blank.

1 A song that tells a story _____

2 A song that was part of a ceremony _____

3 A song that is an old popular hit _____

4 A song that was sung in the early singing-school days _____

5 A song about a great river _____

6 A song that is sung in solo-chorus style _____

7 A song that was sung to make the work easier _____

8 A song that dates back to the American Revolution _____

9 A song whose melody is a favorite with fife and drum corps _____

10 A song that was popular during the Civil War _____

A Amazing Grace
B Paddy Works on the Railway
C Zuni Sunrise Song
D John Henry
E When Johnny Comes Marching Home
F The Girl I Left Behind Me
G Keep in the Middle of the Road
H Roll On, Columbia
I In My Merry Oldsmobile
J Johnny Has Gone for a Soldier

Read each sentence below and, on your worksheet, fill in the blank with the correct word or words from the list below.

steady beat	melodic rhythm
accent mark	mood
tempo	countermelody

1 The speed at which you sing a song is called the _____

2 When you tap your foot in time to the music, you are tapping the _____

3 The music symbol that tells you to sing a note a little louder than the others is called an _____

4 When you clap each note of a song you are clapping the _____

5 A melody that is sung "against" another melody is called a _____

6 When you choose a word that describes the general feeling of a piece of music you are describing the _____

Instruments

When a number is called, read the sentence next to the number. If you think the statement is true, circle the word TRUE. If you think the statement is false, circle the word FALSE. Listen, then circle your answer on your worksheet.

1 Brass instruments are featured.   TRUE   FALSE

2 Brass instruments are featured.   TRUE   FALSE

3 String instruments are featured.   TRUE   FALSE

4 Woodwinds are featured.   TRUE   FALSE

5 The piano plays with the orchestra.   TRUE   FALSE

6 The piano plays alone.   TRUE   FALSE

Steady Beats in Sets

The vertical lines in example 1 represent a series of steady beats. Pat the steady beats on your knees.

1. | | | | | | | | | | | |

The quarter notes in example 2 show a series of 12 steady beats. Pat the steady beats on your knees.

2. ♩ ♩ ♩ ♩ ♩ ♩ ♩ ♩ ♩ ♩ ♩ ♩

Steady beats can be organized into sets. The beats in example 3 are organized in sets of two. Pat the beats in sets of two. Accent the first beat in each set.

3. ♩ ♩ ♩ ♩ ♩ ♩ ♩ ♩ ♩ ♩ ♩ ♩
   >   >   >   >   >   >

In music, sets of beats are separated into measures by bar lines. In example 4 the number 2 at the beginning of the line tells you that there are two beats in each measure. Pat the beats in sets of two. Accent the first beat in each measure.

4. **2** ♩ ♩ | ♩ ♩ | ♩ ♩ | ♩ ♩ | ♩ ♩ | ♩ ♩ |

Pat the beats in sets of two as you listen to this music.

LISTENING SKILLS 3 *Marche militaire* . . . . Schubert

90

Sets of Three

In the lesson on page 90, you learned that beats can be organized into sets. The beats in example 1, below, are organized in sets of three. Pat the beats in sets of three. Accent the first beat in each set.

1. ♩ ♩ ♩ ♩ ♩ ♩ ♩ ♩ ♩ ♩ ♩ ♩
   >   >   >   >

In example 2 the sets of three beats are separated into measures by bar lines. The number 3 at the beginning of the line tells you that there are three beats in each measure. Pat the beats in example 2.

2. **3** ♩ ♩ ♩ | ♩ ♩ ♩ | ♩ ♩ ♩ | ♩ ♩ ♩ |

Meter in 3

This piano piece by Brahms has meter in 3. Feel the beats moving in sets of three as you listen to the recording.

LISTENING SKILLS 3 *Waltz in A Flat Major* . . . . Brahms

Look through your music book to find songs that have meter in 3. Choose one to sing.

Meter in 4

The steady beats keep "moving'" right along in this song.
The number in the color box tells you how the beats are
organized.

Make up a hand pattern that will show the meter of the
song. You can use snaps, claps, taps, or any other hand
sound you can think of. Here is an example.

PAT   snap   snap   snap,   PAT   snap   snap   snap

Movin' Right Along

Words and Music by Paul Williams and Kenny Ascher

1. Mov-in' right a-long__ in search of   good times and   good__ news, With
2. Mov-in' right a-long__ we found a   life on the   high-way And

good friends you can't__ lose, this could be-come a hab-it.
your way is my__ way, so trust my nav-i-ga-tion.

Op-por-tu-ni-ty__ just knocked, let's reach out and grab__ it, To-
Cal-i-for-nia, here__ we come, that pie in the sky__ land.

geth-er we'll nab__ it, we'll hitch-hike, bus, or yel-low cab it.
Palm trees and warm __sand, though sad-ly we just left Rhode Is-land.

Mov-in' right a - long,   foot loose and   fan - cy   free. __
Mov-in' right a - long,   hey L.   A.   where've you   gone? __

Get - tin' there is   half   the   fun; Come   share   it   with   me. __
Send some - one   to   fetch   us, we're in   Sas - katch - e - wan. __

Mov-in' right a - long,   We'll learn to   share   the   load. __
Mov-in' right a - long,   You take it,   you   know   best. __

We don't need   a   map   to keep this   show   on   the   road. __
Hey, I've nev - er   seen   the   sun come   up   in   the   west. __

3. Movin' right along, we're truly birds of a feather,
   We're in this together and you know where you're goin'.
   Movie stars with flashy cars and life with the top down,
   We're stormin' the big town, Yeah! Storm is right, should it be snowing.
   Movin' right along, Do I see signs of man?
   "Welcome" on the same post that says "Come back again."
   Movin' right along, Footloose and fancy free.
   You're ready for the big time. Is it ready for me?

Parts for Percussion

Feel the beats moving in sets of four as you play one of these
instrumental parts to accompany "Movin' Right Along."

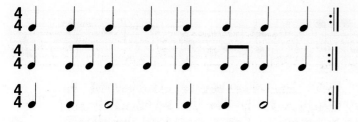

Using the Meter Signature

Look at the numbers in the color box at the beginning of this song. In music those numbers are called a *meter signature*. A meter signature tells you two things.

- The top number tells you that there are three beats in each measure.

- The bottom number tells you that a quarter note (♩) represents one beat.

- Feel the beats in sets of three as you listen to "The Rainbow Connection."

$\frac{3}{4}$ ♩ ♩ ♩ | ♩ ♩ ♩ | ♩ ♩ ♩ | ♩ ♩ ♩ |

The Rainbow Connection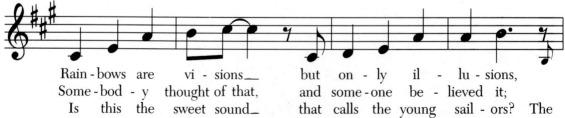

Lyrics and Music by Paul Williams and Kenny Ascher

1. Why are there so man-y songs a-bout rain-bows, and
2. Who said that ev-'ry wish would be heard and an-swered when
3. Have you been half a-sleep and have you heard voic-es?

what's on the oth - er side? _____
wished on the morn - ing star? _____
I've heard them calling my name. _____

Rain-bows are vi - sions___ but on-ly il - lu-sions,
Some-bod-y thought of that, and some-one be - lieved it;
Is this the sweet sound___ that calls the young sail-ors? The

rain - bows have noth - ing to hide. _____
Look what it's done ___ so far. _____
voice might be one and the same. _____

So we've been told and some choose to be - lieve it; _____
What's so a - maz - ing that keeps us star - gaz - ing And
I've heard it too man - y times to ig - nore it It's

I know they're wrong; wait and see, _____
what do we think we might see? _____
some - thing that I'm s'posed to be. _____

Some - day we'll find it, The Rain - bow Con - nec - tion; The

lov - ers, the dream - ers, ___ and me. _____

Parts for Percussion

Feel the beats moving in sets of three as you play one of
these instrumental parts to accompany "The Rainbow
Connection."

Review: Conducting the Meter

Meter in 2

In $\frac{2}{4}$ meter the strong beat is the first of a group of two steady beats. Play beats in sets of two on a woodblock. Make the first beat of each set stronger than the other.

Try the conducting pattern for meter in 2. Think *1 2, 1 2,* as you make the motions.

The following songs have meter in 2. Choose one of them and conduct class singing.

- Nelly Bly, p. 50
- I Like It Here, p. 222
- Johnny's My Boy, p. 66

Meter in 3

In $\frac{3}{4}$ meter the strong beat is the first of a group of three steady beats. Play the beats in sets of three on a drum. Make the first beat of each set stronger than the others.

Try the conducting pattern for meter in 3. Think *1 2 3,*
1 2 3, as you make the motions.

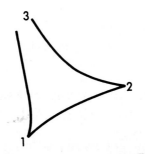

The following songs have meter in 3. Choose one of them and
conduct class singing.

- America, p. 220
- Roll On, Columbia, p. 42
- The Sidewalks of New York, p. 52

Meter in 4

In $\frac{4}{4}$ meter the strong beat is the first of a group of four
steady beats. Play beats in sets of four on a tambourine.
Make the first beat of each set stronger than the others.

Try the conducting pattern for meter in 4. Think *1 2 3 4,*
1 2 3 4, as you make the motions.

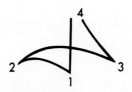

The following songs have meter in 4. Choose one of them and
conduct class singing.

- Over the Meadow, p. 142
- Come, Ye Thankful People, Come, p. 231
- America, the Beautiful, p. 221

Changing Meters

Sometimes a composer uses more than one meter in a song. Look through the song "Rain" on the next page. What two meter signatures do you find?

Practice Patterns

Clapping these patterns will help you get ready to sing a song with changing meters.

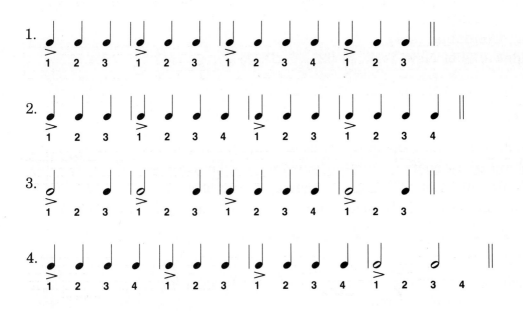

Challenge Patterns

Here are three challenge patterns. Can you clap one of them? All three?

Rain

Words by Annie W. McCullough   Music by Paul Hindemith

You will hear the meter change from $\frac{2}{4}$ to $\frac{3}{4}$ to $\frac{2}{4}$ all through this old German folk song.

My Joy Would Grow in Measure . . . . **Fifteenth-Century Song**

$\frac{6}{8}$ Meter

In $\frac{6}{8}$ meter the strong beat is the first of a group of six steady beats. Clap beats in sets of six. Make the first beat in each set stronger than the others.

A conductor uses this pattern for meter in 6. Try it. Think *1 2 3 4 5 6* as you make the motions.

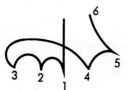

Use the conducting pattern to keep time to this music that moves in $\frac{6}{8}$ meter.

 On Hearing the First Cuckoo in Spring . . . . . Delius

Tempo Makes a Difference

When music written in $\frac{6}{8}$ meter is performed at a fast tempo, the conductor feels the music moving in twos and shows only the first and fourth beats.

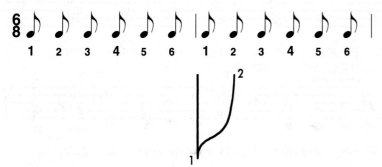

Try conducting this music. It moves in a fast $\frac{6}{8}$ meter.

 Sonata in F . . . . Handel

100

⁶⁄₈ Meter: Slow or Fast?

As you listen to "Viva L'Amour," clap your hands lightly to
keep time to the music.

Viva L'Amour

College Song

2. Come all ye good ladies and join in the song, . . .
   Sing out with bright voices and help it along, . . .

3. A friend on the left and a friend on the right, . . .
   A song of good friendship we're singing tonight, . . .

Rhythm: Even and Uneven

Here are the beginnings of four songs that you may know. Each one is written two ways. How is the second line of music (b) different from the first line (a)?

Listen for even and uneven patterns in the Irish ballad on the next page. Follow the music as you listen.

The Gypsy Rover

Irish Folk Song

1. The gyp - sy ro - ver came o - ver the hill, Bound through the val - ley so shad - y. He whis - tled and he sang till the green woods rang, — And he won the heart of a la - dy.

REFRAIN

Ly - de - o, ly - de - o, da - day, Ly - de - o, Ly - de - ay - de; He whis - tled and he sang till the green woods rang, — And he won the heart of a la - dy.

2. She left her father's castle gate,
   Left her own true lover,
   She left her servants and her estate
   To follow the gypsy rover. *(Refrain)*

3. Her father saddled his fastest steed,
   Rode by the river Clayde,
   Drew near to a mansion with great speed,
   Found the gypsy and his lady. *(Refrain)*

4. "He's no gypsy, my father," said she,
   "But lord of the freelands all over,
   And I will stay till my dying day
   With my whistling gypsy rover." *(Refrain)*

Melody—A Line of Sounds

A melody is a line of single tones that repeat or that move upward and downward by step or by leap.

How the tones move is one of the things that makes one melody different from another. Here are four examples from songs in your book. Each one shows how tones can move.

How do the tones move in the song on the next page? Follow the music as you listen.

Can you identify how the tones move in each color box?

The Greatest American Hero

Words by Stephen Geyer   Music by Mike Post

1. Look at what hap - pened to me,
2. Just like the light _ of a new _ day _   It

I can't be - lieve _ it, my - self,
hit me from out _ of the blue, _

Sud - den - ly I'm _ up on top of the world, _   It
Break - ing me out _ of the spell I was in, _ mak - ing

should have been some - bod - y else. _
all of my wish - es come true. _

Be - lieve it or not, I'm walk - in' on air _

I nev - er thought I could feel _ so free, _

Fly - in' a - way _ on a wing _ and a pray'r, _

who could _ it be? _   Be - lieve it or not _ it's just me.

Steps, Leaps, or Repeats?

All of the music examples below have something in common. Can you discover what it is?

Notice that in each example, some notes are set off in brackets. How do those notes move?

Try to play each of the examples on bells. Pay particular attention to the *sound* of the pattern when you play the notes in the brackets.

Melody Patterns that Step

In this song there are two melody patterns that move first downward and then upward by step. Can you find them?

Rise Up, O Flame

Words and Music by Christoph Praetorius

Rise up, O flame, _____ By _ thy _ light glow - ing,

Show to us beau - ty, _ vi - sion, _ and joy.

When your class is familiar with the melody of "Rise Up, O Flame," you will be able to sing the song as a two- or three-part round.

Add an Accompaniment

Here are four accompaniment parts to play when "Rise Up, O Flame" is sung as a round. Can you describe how the tones move in each part?

Different Scale, Different Sound

On the recording you will hear two versions of "Alleluia, Amen." Do they *sound* the same or different?

Alleluia, Amen

Traditional Round

The two versions sound different because the music in each version is based on a different scale.

The word *scale* comes from the Italian word *scala,* which means "ladder." This is a good word to use, because when notes are arranged on the staff in a scale pattern, they appear to be climbing a ladder.

Version 1 of "Alleluia, Amen" is based on this scale. Play it several times on the bells.

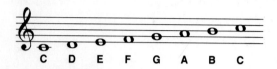

Version 2 of "Alleluia, Amen" is based on this scale. Play it several times on the bells.

Why Scales Sound Different

Half Steps and Whole Steps

It is important to understand half steps and whole steps because they are the building blocks of much of the music we hear today.

Start anywhere on the piano keyboard and play every key, first moving in an upward direction, then in a downward direction. Don't skip any black or white keys. You will be playing *half steps*.

The distance between *any* two keys with a single key between them is called a *whole step*. Start anywhere on the keyboard and play whole steps.

Major and Minor Scales

Whole steps and half steps can be arranged to form different scales. Here is a *major scale* starting on C. Arrange the bells to match the diagram, and notice the pattern of whole steps and half steps. Play this major scale upward and downward to hear its special sound.

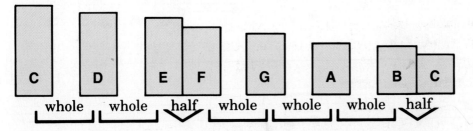

Here is a *minor scale* starting on C. It will sound different from the C-major scale because the pattern of whole steps and half steps is different. Arrange the bells to match the diagram. Then play this minor scale upward and downward to hear its special sound.

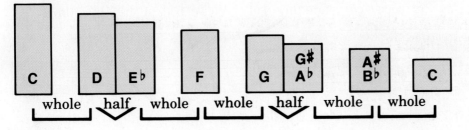

Phrases and Cadences

There are six phrases in this song. Each one is marked
with a phrase line. Trace the rise and fall of the phrase
lines as you listen to "A Round of Goodbyes."

A Round of Goodbyes

Words and Music by Frederick Silver

Good - bye,   fare - well;   The   time has come   for   part - ing.

Take   care,   stay   well;   I'll   see you   in   a   while.

We have had a lot of hap-py mem-o-ries, And I guess we've had a lot of   fun;

And I hope the mem-o-ries will lin-ger on Now that we're through and   done.

Good - bye, *au re-voir, ciao,* fare thee well, We've had a hap-py time.

Good - bye, *au re-voir, ciao,* fare thee well, See you a - gain.

Follow the Phrase Diagram

When you sing the melody of "A Round of Goodbyes," you will notice that it is natural to take a breath at the end of each phrase. The pauses in the flow of the melody are called *cadences*.

Look at the phrase diagram below. Notice the words at the end of each line.

- A *weak cadence* gives an "unfinished" feeling—as though there is more music to come.
- A *strong cadence* gives a feeling of coming to a "resting place"—the music seems finished or complete.

Trace the phrase lines as you sing the song.

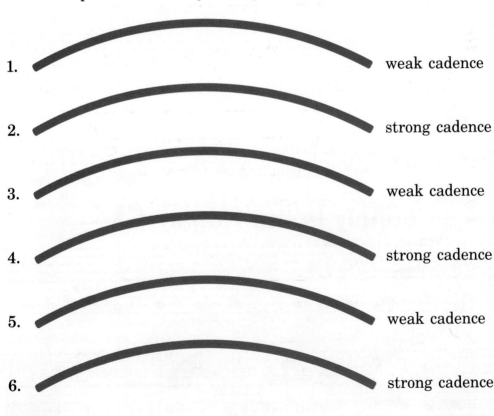

1. weak cadence

2. strong cadence

3. weak cadence

4. strong cadence

5. weak cadence

6. strong cadence

Listen for the cadences in this music.

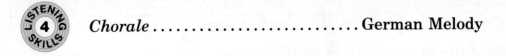

Chorale . . . . German Melody

Register—Range

In music, highness and lowness of sound is called *register*. If a group of tones are all high sounds, they are in a high register. If a group of tones are all low sounds, they are in a low register.

In this music you will hear sounds that are mostly high, mostly low, and both high and low at the same time.

 "Samuel Goldenberg and Schmuyle" from *Pictures at an Exhibition* .... Mussorgsky

In a melody the span from the lowest tone to the highest tone is called *range*. The range may be narrow or wide.

Narrow range   Wide range

Look at the music of this Navajo Indian song. The lowest note is shown in the color box. Find the highest note.

Lonely Is the Hogan 4

Translated by Derrick N. Lehmer   Navajo Indian Song

1. Lone - ly   is   the   ho - gan, _____ The   birds   are   still.
2. White   up - on   the   me - sa _____ The   win - ter   snow,

No   more _ the wild   flow - ers bloom   on   the   hill.
Cold   blows _ the wind   through _ the   can - yon   be - low.

Courtesy of Eunice M. Lehmer. From SONGS OF THE MESA by Derrick Norman Lehmer.

Is the range of the song narrow or wide?

Narrow Range—Wide Range

Clap your hands or tap your toes in time to the music of
"Every Mornin'." Sing along when you can.

Every Mornin' ④

Words and Music by Avon Gillespie

Finding the Range

Look at the music of "Lonely Is the Hogan" on page 112. Does
the melody have an 8-note range? A 4-note range? A 6-note
range?

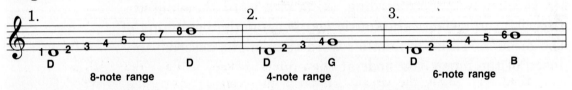

What is the range of the melody in "Every Mornin'"? Is the
range narrow or wide? To find out, count the notes from the
lowest to the highest.

An Opera Prelude

EL JALEO
JOHN SINGER SARGENT

Many people think that Georges Bizet's opera *Carmen* is one of the most exciting operas of all times. Its plot is full of colorful characters—smugglers and bullfighters, soldiers and gypsies. Before the curtain rises, the orchestra plays the "Prelude," with music that sets the mood of the story that follows.

As you listen to the recording, think of a word that might describe the mood of the music you hear at the beginning of the prelude. Think of another word that might describe the mood of the music you hear at the end.

 "Prelude" from *Carmen* . . . . Bizet

Here are the three main themes Bizet used in the "Prelude" to *Carmen*. If you are a piano player, you might want to play each theme before you listen to the recording again.

Georges Bizet
(1838–1875)

From early childhood, Georges Bizet showed a great interest in music; he learned the musical scale along with his alphabet. When he was nine years old, he entered the Paris Conservatory. He was an outstanding student and won many prizes for his piano playing and his compositions.

Throughout his life, Bizet was most interested in writing music for the stage. His opera *Carmen* is considered one of the great operas of all times, and today most opera houses around the world feature this popular work.

One Way to Make Harmony

Clap the steady beat as you listen to this work song from Israel. Sing along on the nonsense syllables in section A.

Zum Gali Gali

Folk Song from Israel

A E MIN

Zum ga - li ga - li, ga - li, Zum ga - li ga - li,

E MIN *Fine*

Zum ga - li ga - li, ga - li, Zum ga - li ga - li.

B E MIN

1. Pi - o - neers work hard on the land, _____
2. As they la - bor all day _____ long, _____

E MIN *D.C. al Fine*

— Men and wom - en work hand in hand.
— They _____ lift their voice in _____ song.

116

Sing an Ostinato

One way to add harmony to a melody is to sing an *ostinato*—
a melody pattern that repeats. Follow the ostinato pattern
in the music below as you listen to another version of
"Zum Gali Gali."

Play an Ostinato

Here are three instrumental ostinatos to add to a
performance of "Zum Gali Gali."

Partner Songs

Listen to the spirituals on this page and the next. Follow the music as each song is played, and sing along when you can.

This Train

Black Spiritual

1. This train is bound for glory, this train, __
This train is bound for glory, this train, __
This train is bound for glory, If you ride it you must be holy,
This train is bound for glory, this train. __

2. This train don't pull no sleepers, this train,
This train don't pull no sleepers, this train,
This train don't pull no sleepers,
Don't pull nothin' but the righteous people,
This train don't pull no sleepers, this train.

3. This train don't take your money, this train,
This train don't take your money, this train,
This train don't take your money,
Pay your way with milk and honey,
This train don't take your money, this train.

Collected and adapted by John A. Lomax and Alan Lomax. TRO—© Copyright 1934 and renewed 1962 Ludlow Music, Inc., New York, N.Y. Used by permission.

When the Saints Go Marching In

Black Spiritual

1. Oh, when the saints _____ go march-ing in, _____ Oh, when the
saints go march - ing in, _____ Oh, Lord I
want to be in that num - ber _____ When the
saints go march - ing in.

2. Oh, when the stars refuse to shine,
Oh, when the stars refuse to shine,
Oh, Lord, I want to be in that number
When the stars refuse to shine.

3. Oh, when I hear that trumpet sound, . . .

Singing in Harmony

While some of your classmates sing "This Train," others can
sing "When the Saints Go Marching In."

When two different songs are sung at the same time, they
are called *partner songs.* Singing partner songs is an easy
way to create harmony.

Countermelodies

There are two different melodies in this song. Each one is written on a separate staff, and each one is identified by a different color box. Follow one of the melodies as you listen to the recording. The color boxes will help you keep your place.

Swinging Along 5

Traditional

How Countermelodies Work

Melody lines may be tunes by themselves.

Two melody lines may be sung together to create harmony.

When two melody lines are sung or played together, they are called *countermelodies*.

Melody and Descant

You can create harmony by adding a *descant* to a melody.
A descant is a kind of countermelody that often soars high
above the main melody of a song. Listen for the descant in
the recording of "Streets of Laredo." In some verses it is
played on an instrument. In others it is sung.

Streets of Laredo

American Cowboy Song

DESCANT

Slow,   slow,   bang   the drum   slow,

Melody

1. As   I ____ walked   out   in   the   streets   of   La - re - do,
2. "I   see   by your   out - fit   that   you   are   a   cow - boy,"

Bang   the drum   slow,   Bang   the drum   slow.

As   I   walked   out   in   La - re - do   one   day,
These   words   he   said   as   I   bold - ly   walked   by;

122

3. "Now once in the saddle I used to ride handsome,
'A handsome young cowboy' is what they would say.
I'd ride into town and go down to the card-house,
But I'm shot in the chest and I'm dying today.

4. "Go run to the spring for a cup of cold water
To cool down my fever," the young cowboy said.
But when I returned, his poor soul had departed,
And I wept when I saw the young cowboy was dead.

5. We'll bang the drum slowly and play the fife lowly,
We'll play the dead march as we bear him along.
We'll go to the graveyard and lay the sod o'er him;
He was a young cowboy, but he had done wrong.

Listen for the melody of "Streets of Laredo" in this piano
piece by an American composer—Roy Harris.

"Streets of Laredo" from
American Ballads .... Harris

Two-Part Harmony

Follow the music as you listen to the recording of "The *John B.* Sails." Notice that for the most part, the bottom line of notes follows the contour of the melody.

The *John B.* Sails

Folk Song from the Bahama Islands

1. Oh, we come on the sloop *John* *B.* My grand - fa - ther and me, A - round Nas - sau Town we did roam. Walk - in' all night Just see - in' the sights, Well, I feel so break up, I want to go home.

2. The first mate he got sad, Feel - in' aw - f'ly bad, Captain come a - board, took him a - way. Please let me a - lone And let me go home, Well, I feel so break up, I want to go home.

3. The poor cook he got fits, And throw way all the grits, Then he took and eat up all of the corn. Please let me go home, I want to go home, Well, this is the worst trip Since I was born.

REFRAIN

So hoist up ___ the *John B.* sails,

See how ___ the main - s'l set, Send for ___ the Cap - t'n a -

shore, Let ___ me go home. Please let ___ me go

home, I want ___ to go home. Well, ___ I

feel so break ___ up, ___ I want ___ to go home.

Harmonic Intervals

In two-part harmony the distance between the bottom note
and top note is called a *harmonic interval*.

We can name the interval by calling the bottom note *1* and
counting up to the top note.

125

Playing Chords

Harmony is created when autoharp chords are added to a melody. Use the F, C₇, and B♭ chords to add harmony to one of these songs.

- This Train, p. 118
- When the Saints Go Marching In, p. 119
- Roll On, Columbia, p. 42
- Laredo, p. 72

Each of the chords used to accompany the songs listed above is built on a tone of the F-major scale. The tone on which each chord is built is called the *root*.

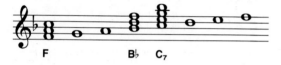

The separate tones in each chord are notated below. Play each example on the bells.

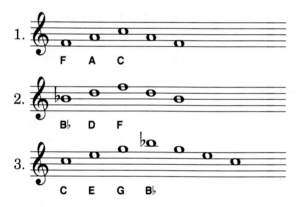

With two other classmates, play chords on the bells. Which part will you play?

126

Three-Part Harmony

The harmony in "Kum Ba Yah" is based on the F, B♭, and C₇ chords. In the lesson on page 126, you played those chords on the autoharp and on the bells. Listen for voices singing the chords on the recording of this song.

Kum Ba Yah

Traditional Song from South Africa

1. Someone's singin', Lord, Kum ba yah! . . .
   Oh, Lord, Kum ba yah!

2. Someone's prayin', Lord, Kum ba yah! . . .
   Oh, Lord, Kum ba yah!

3. Someone's shoutin', Lord, Kum ba yah! . . .
   Oh, Lord, Kum ba yah!

4. Kum ba yah, my Lord, Kum ba yah! . . .
   Oh, Lord, Kum ba yah!

Two Sections, A and B

This song has two different sections. The letters A and B in the score will help you see the beginning and end of sections. To show that you hear two different sections in the song, clap the beat during section A and snap the beat during section B.

Harmony ⑤

Words and Music by Norman Simon and Artie Kaplan

1. The time has come, Let us be-gin, with all our voic-es
2. Like the shep-herd guards his sheep, ⁊ Watch your chil-dren

join-ing in, _____ To sing of love and broth-er-hood, __
as they sleep, __ And like the pot-ter turns his clay, __

And peo-ple do-ing what they should to help their fel-low
Oh, help us shape a bet-ter day and let us sing a

Contrasting Sections

Can you hear the contrasts between section A and
section B? The words are different; the melodies are
different. What other differences can you discover between
the sections of "Harmony"?

ABA Form

This song, like the song "Harmony" on page 128, has two
different sections—A and B. But in "There's a Meeting
Here Tonight," one of the sections is repeated. Listen to
the song to discover which section is repeated.

There's a Meeting Here Tonight

Black Spiritual

B *Solo*   *Chorus*

1. Camp meet-ing in the wil-der-ness,
2. Come join us in the wil-der-ness, There's a meet-ing here to-night.
3. We'll praise Him in the wil-der-ness,

Solo   *Chorus*

Camp meet-ing in the wil-der-ness,
We'll hear a-bout e-ter-nal rest, There's a meet-ing here to-night.
Lift up your voice and shout with us,

A *Chorus*

Get you read-y, There's a meet-ing here to-night, Come a-long —

there's a meet-ing here to-night; I know you by your

dai - ly walk, There's a meet-ing here to - night.

Check the Form

Many of the songs in your book have two contrasting
sections. Some of the songs are in AB form; others are in
ABA form. Look through the songs listed below. Which are
in AB form? Which are in ABA form?

- Sweet Betsy from Pike, p. 34
- Ev'ry Time I Feel the Spirit, p. 18
- The Sidewalks of New York, p. 52
- What Would the World Be Like Without Music? p. 4
- Blow the Wind Southerly, p. 70
- Keep in the Middle of the Road, p. 20

Three Different Sections

A B A C A

The shapes and letters at the top of the page show you how three different sections of a song are put together into a form called *rondo*. Which section repeats?

The Rondo Song

Words and Music by Linda Williams

A A ron-do, a ron-do, it runs a-round a track.

The theme called "A" will go a-way, but it will be right back!

And ev-'ry-bo-dy knows that's how a ron-do __ goes.

B Then comes a theme called "B" in an-oth-er style and

once in a while in an-oth-er key. That's how you know it's "B."

A And then the ron-do, the ron-do comes back a-round the track.

The theme called "A" will go a - way, but it will be right back!

And ev - 'ry - bo - dy knows that's how a ron - do __ goes.

Now for an - oth - er theme, Now for an - oth - er sound,

This time we call it "C," a mel - o - dy that comes a - round

to the ron - do, the ron - do, it runs a - round a track.

The theme called "A" has gone a - way, but sure e - nough, it's back!

And ev - 'ry - bo - dy knows that's how a ron - do __ goes.

Coda

That's the way it goes!

Call Chart 2   **Rondo Form**

Follow the chart as you listen. It will help you hear how
the sections of this ragtime music are put together to
create a rondo form.

5 *Cotton Boll Rag* ....Hunter

1 INTRODUCTION

2 SECTION A

3 SECTION B

4 SECTION A

5 SECTION C

6 SECTION A

Rondo Form

Here is another piece in rondo form. Listen for this theme every time section A returns.

Allegro . . . . Beethoven

1 SECTION A

2 SECTION B

3 SECTION A

4 SECTION C

5 SECTION A

6 SECTION B

7 SECTON A

8 CODA

Theme and Variations

What is the subject, or theme, of the pictures shown above?
How has the subject been changed to make each picture look
different?

A Musical Theme

A familiar melody can be used as a musical theme. Play
this one on the bells. Do you recognize the tune?

A theme can be changed so that it sounds different. Can
you think of a way to change, or vary, the theme that you
played?

On the next page you will find four variations on the
familiar-tune theme. Can you discover how the theme has
been changed to make each variation sound different?

Four Variations

Variation 1

Fine
D.C. al Fine

Variation 2

Fine
D.C. al Fine

Variation 3

Fine
D.C. al Fine

Variation 4

Fine
D.C. al Fine

Same Theme, Different Styles

In the following piano piece, you will hear how Mozart used the same familiar tune in one of his compositions.

LISTENING SKILLS 6 *Variations on "Ah, vous dirai-je Maman"*... Mozart

Here is another set of variations on the same theme.

LISTENING SKILLS 6 *Variations on a Nursery Song* .... Dohnanyi

A Musical Giant

You will hear an example of music by Johann Sebastian Bach—
a composer who is considered to be one of the greatest
composers who ever lived. The music you will hear is the last
movement of Bach's *Brandenburg Concerto No. 2*. It is scored
for four different solo instruments, which are accompanied by
strings and harpsichord.

As you listen, try to answer the following questions:

• Is the beat strong and steady?
• Is the tempo fast or slow?
• Is the music lively or serene?
• Can you identify any of the solo instruments?

 Brandenburg Concerto No. 2, Movement 3.... Bach

This rhythm pattern is used over and over again. Try clapping
it or tapping it on your desk.

Listen for this theme. Can you hear it as it is played by each
solo instrument? When is it played by the low strings in the
accompaniment part?

**Johann Sebastian
Bach**
(1685–1750)

When Johann Sebastian Bach was born,
the Bach family had been musicians for
over 250 years. All the members of this
large German family could sing or play
the harpsichord, organ, or violin. Johann
Sebastian was no exception. As soon as
his hands were big enough to hold a violin, his father began to teach him to play.
But it was the organ that became Johann
Sebastian's favorite instrument.

For many years, Bach was the choir
leader and organist of Saint Thomas's
Church in the city of Leipzig. This German city was the center for great fairs
that brought crowds of people to the city
every year. As a result, the fame of Bach
as an organist and a composer spread all
through Germany. Today he is hailed
throughout the world as one of the greatest composers of all time.

The Sound of Voices

Your voice has a special sound (tone color), whether you use it to whisper, speak, shout, or sing. Every person in the world has a voice that sounds different from any other voice.

If there were 25 students in your class and each one read the following statement aloud, you would hear 25 different vocal tone colors. Try it.

My voice is an individual possession. No one else in the world has a voice that sounds exactly like mine.

Listen for the voices on the recording of "For the Beauty of the Earth." Who is singing?

For the Beauty of the Earth

Words by Folliott S. Pierpoint   Music by Conrad Kocher

1. For the — beau - ty of the earth, For the beau - ty
2. For the — beau - ty of each hour Of the day and
3. For the — joy of hu - man love, Broth - er, sis - ter,

of the skies, For the — love which from our birth
of the night, Hill and — vale and tree and flower,
par - ent, child, Friends on — earth and friends a - bove,

O - ver and a - round us lies,
Sun and moon and stars of light, Lord of all, to
For all gen - tle thoughts and mild,

Thee we raise This our hymn of grate - ful praise.

A Quartet of Voices

Listen for the voices on this recording of "For the Beauty of the Earth." Do you hear men's voices, women's voices, or both?

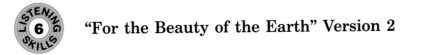 **"For the Beauty of the Earth" Version 2**

Adult singers are grouped according to the tone color and register (highness or lowness) of their voices.

- Soprano: high, woman's voice
- Alto: low, woman's voice
- Tenor: high, man's voice
- Bass: low, man's voice

As you listen to the recording again, try following one of the voice parts. Will you follow the soprano, alto, tenor, or bass part?

For the beau-ty of the earth, For the glo-ry of the skies,

For the love which from our birth O - ver and a - round us lies:

Lord of all, to Thee we raise This our hymn of grate-ful praise.

Vocal Ensembles

Duet

Music that is written for two performers to sing or play in harmony is called a *duet*. Any combination of two performers can sing a duet—a boy and a girl, a man and a woman, two boys, two girls, and so forth.

"Over the Meadow" is arranged for two voices. Listen to the recording. What combination of voices do you hear?

When you know the song, team up with a friend and try singing "Over the Meadow" as a duet.

Over the Meadow

Czech Folk Song   Translated by Adolph C. Topinka
English Version Adapted by Linda Williams

1. O - ver the mea - dow, gold and green
2. Spy - ing them from the cas - tle walls,

Grass - es are grow - ing, grass - es are grow - ing,

Two lone - ly maid - ens can be seen,
"Come, sad - dle up!" the mas - ter calls,

Sad - ly they walk the coun - try - side. *Hey!*
"We shall go hunt - ing, off we'll ride!"

Oh, how the wa-ters flow, Pure as my heart they go

Down from the win-ter snow, circ-ling the ma-ple tree, —

Oh, how the ri-vers flow, Strong as my heart they go

Down from the win-ter snow, circ-ling to me. *Hey!*

3. "Master, your gun!" the servant cries,
   Grasses are growing, grasses are growing,
   "I shall not need it" he replies,
   "One lovely maid will be my bride." *(Refrain)*

Trio

Music that is written for three performers to sing or play in harmony is called a *trio*. Any combination of three performers can sing a trio—two women and a man, three women, three men, and so forth.

As you listen to the selections listed below, think about these two things.
- What combination of voices do you hear in each piece?
- Are the pieces in the same style, or are they in different styles?

The Alphabet . . . . Mozart

Boogie Woogie Bugle Boy . . . . Prince/Raye

Quartets in Close Harmony

Here is an old song that was popular during the Civil War days. Listen for the voices on the recording. Are they singing in unison or in harmony? Are the voices accompanied by instruments or is there no accompaniment?

Aura Lee

Words by W. W. Fosdick   Music by George R. Poulton

1. As the black-bird in the spring 'Neath the wil-low tree
2. On her cheek the rose was born, Mu-sic when she spoke.

Sat and piped, I heard him sing, sing-ing Au-ra Lee.
In her eyes the rays of morn In-to splen-dor broke.

REFRAIN

Au - ra Lee, Au-ra Lee, maid with gold-en hair!

Sun-shine came a-long with thee, And swal-lows in the air.

Listen for the voices in this recording of "Aura Lee." What do you hear?

 *Aura Lee* . . . . **Poulton**

In this recording, you will hear another group of voices singing in close harmony. Can you tell who is singing?

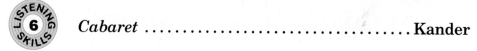 *Cabaret* . . . . **Kander**

Instrumental Ensembles

There was a time when there were no public concerts to attend, no radio or record players to listen to, and no television to watch. In those days, if people wanted to enjoy music, they had to make their own.

It was not uncommon for small groups of friends to gather at a home and make music for their own pleasure. The music that these small groups of instrumentalists played came to be known as chamber music because it was performed in a room, or chamber, rather than in a large concert hall.

Some of the world's greatest music was written for chamber ensembles and chamber music is still being composed today.

Each selection listed below was written for a small instrumental ensemble. As you listen to each piece, try to answer these questions:

• Is the music performed by two players (duet)? By three players (trio)? By four players (quartet)?

• What instruments do you hear? Woodwinds? Brasses? Strings?

 "Scherzo" from *Grand Sonata in A Major*..Giuliani

 Concerto in G Minor ....Vivaldi

 "Dance" from *Folk Suite* ....Mitchell

 Canzonetta.........................Mendelssohn

HAYDN REHEARSING A STRING QUARTET AS IMAGINED BY A 19TH CENTURY ARTIST

STRING QUARTETTE
JACK LEVINE

A Symphony by Beethoven

The conductor's score below shows the first eight measures of Beethoven's *Symphony No. 1,* Movement 3. What does the score tell you about

- The tempo?
- The dynamics?
- The instruments that will play?

Here are three themes that Beethoven used in *Symphony No. 1*, Movement 3. If you are a piano player, you might want to play each theme before you listen to the recording.

Theme 1

Theme 2

Theme 3

Symphony No. 1, Movement 3 . . . . Beethoven

Ludwig van Beethoven
(1770–1827)

Ludwig van Beethoven was born into a poor but musical family. His father was his first teacher. The young Beethoven began to study piano when he was four years old. He played in public when he was eight, and by the time he was eleven, he had written and published three piano sonatas. A few years later, Beethoven went to Vienna. The music lovers of that Austrian city soon recognized Beethoven's amazing ability as a pianist and later appreciated his genius as a composer.

No one knows exactly when Beethoven wrote his *Symphony No. 1*. We do know, however, that it was given its first performance in Vienna on April 2, 1800. We also know that Beethoven himself conducted the performance.

Call Chart 4

Following the chart will help you hear what is going on as the music goes along.

 Symphony No. 1, Movement 3..........Beethoven

1 Theme 1 in violins; repeated rhythm pattern (♩ ♩ ♩) in low strings; ◁ builds up from *p* to *f* ; all repeated

2 Theme 2 in violins; rhythmic figure (𝄾 ♩ ♩) in woodwinds and low strings; ♩ ♩ ♩ pattern continues over repeated melody pattern in low strings

3 Theme 1 returns in violins and woodwinds; short ending section (coda) with bits of melody in violins, punctuated with chords in woodwinds, brass, and low strings; builds up to *ff* with woodwinds, brass, and strings playing in unison

4 Call 2 repeated

5 Call 3 repeated

6 Theme 3 in woodwinds, alternating with rapid scale patterns in strings; section ends with chords in woodwinds and brass, with scale patterns in violins

7 Call 6 repeated

8 Theme 1 in violins; repeated rhythm pattern (♩ ♩ ♩) in low strings; ⎯⎯ builds up from p to f

9 Theme 2 in violins; rhythmic figure (𝄾 ♩ ♩) in woodwinds and low strings; ♩ ♩ ♩ pattern continues over repeated melody pattern in low strings

10 Theme 1 returns in violins and woodwinds; short ending section (coda) with bits of melody in violins, punctuated with chords in woodwinds, brass, and low strings; building up to ff with woodwinds, brass, and strings playing in unison

Careers in Music

H. Robert Reynolds talks about his career as teacher and conductor.

LISTENING SKILLS 7

Careers in Music—
H. Robert Reynolds

You will hear seven songs from your book. As you listen to each song, decide whether the beats are moving in a meter of 2 or a meter of 3. Listen, then circle your answer on your worksheet.

1 METER IN 2   METER IN 3

2 METER IN 2   METER IN 3

3 METER IN 2   METER IN 3

4 METER IN 2   METER IN 3

5 METER IN 2   METER IN 3

6 METER IN 2   METER IN 3

7 METER IN 2   METER IN 3

Test 3 ✓

1 On your worksheet, draw bar lines that will organize this line of quarter notes into sets of two. Write the correct meter signature at the beginning of the line.

♩ ♩ ♩ ♩ ♩ ♩ ♩ ♩ ♩ ♩ ♩ ♩

2 Draw bar lines that will organize this line of quarter notes into sets of three. Write the correct meter signature at the beginning of the line.

♩ ♩ ♩ ♩ ♩ ♩ ♩ ♩ ♩ ♩ ♩ ♩

3 Draw bar lines that will organize this line of quarter notes into sets of four. Write the correct meter signature at the beginning of the line.

♩ ♩ ♩ ♩ ♩ ♩ ♩ ♩ ♩ ♩ ♩ ♩

This note-value chart will help you answer questions 4–6.

Write your answers in the blanks.

4 How many quarter notes can take the place of a half note? _____

5 How many eighth notes can take the place of a quarter note? _____

6 How many quarter notes can take the place of a dotted-half note? _____

A. Look at the meter signature in each example below. On
   your worksheet, draw in the missing bar lines.

1

2

3

B. Fill in the missing meter signature in each example
   below. Will the meter signature be $\frac{2}{4}$, $\frac{3}{4}$, or $\frac{4}{4}$?

1

2

3

4

You will hear parts of seven instrumental pieces. Each time a number is called, decide whether the music moves in a meter of 2 or a meter of 3. Listen, then circle your answer on your worksheet.

1   METER IN 2   METER IN 3

2   METER IN 2   METER IN 3

3   METER IN 2   METER IN 3

4   METER IN 2   METER IN 3

5   METER IN 2   METER IN 3

6   METER IN 2   METER IN 3

7   METER IN 2   METER IN 3

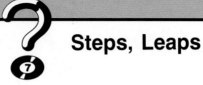
You will hear seven themes. Each one is from a different symphony. As you listen to each theme, decide whether the tones move mostly by step or mostly by leap. Listen, then circle your answer on your worksheet.

1   STEP   LEAP

2   STEP   LEAP

3   STEP   LEAP

4   STEP   LEAP

5   STEP   LEAP

6   STEP   LEAP

7   STEP   LEAP

What Do You Hear? 6 — Major, Minor

You will hear seven songs from your book. As you listen to each song, decide whether the music is based on a major scale or a minor scale. Listen, then circle your answer on your worksheet.

1	MAJOR	MINOR
2	MAJOR	MINOR
3	MAJOR	MINOR
4	MAJOR	MINOR
5	MAJOR	MINOR
6	MAJOR	MINOR
7	MAJOR	MINOR

What Do You Hear? 7 — Tonality

Listen to this piece for orchestra. Each time a number is called, choose the word that describes the tonality. Is it major, or minor? Listen, then circle your answer on your worksheet.

1	MAJOR	MINOR
2	MAJOR	MINOR
3	MAJOR	MINOR

Can you hear the changes in tonality in this piece for orchestra? Each time a number is called, choose the word that describes the tonality. Listen, then circle your answer on your worksheet.

1	MAJOR	MINOR
2	MAJOR	MINOR
3	MAJOR	MINOR

Test 5

A. On your worksheet, circle the lowest and highest notes in each melody below. Then use the blank staff at the end of each melody to show the range. Before you begin, look at the example.

Example

B. Which melody has the widest range? Write the number of the melody in the blank. _____

Which melody has the narrowest range? Write the number of the melody in the blank. _____

These letters and words show the form of some songs in your book

AB   ABA   ABACA coda   AABA coda   AABB coda

Each song listed below is written in one of the forms shown above. Look through the music. Then, on your worksheet, write the name of the form in the blank. Use the song index in your book to find the page number of each song.

1. Sweet Betsy from Pike _____

2. Ev'ry Time I Feel the Spirit _____

3. Blow the Wind Southerly _____

4. The Sidewalks of New York _____

5. This Little Light of Mine _____

6. Lady of the Air _____

7. Keep in the Middle of the Road _____

8. Evening of Roses _____

9. Let's Go Singin' _____

10. The Rondo Song _____

What Do You Hear? 8

Tone Color

You will hear six examples of ensembles. In some examples you will hear a small instrumental group, in others, a small vocal group. When a number is called, choose the word or words that describe what you hear. Listen, then circle your answer on your worksheet.

1

STRING ENSEMBLE   BRASS ENSEMBLE   WOODWIND ENSEMBLE

2

STRING ENSEMBLE   BRASS ENSEMBLE   WOODWIND ENSEMBLE

3

WOMEN'S VOICES   MEN'S VOICES   COMBINATION

4

STRING ENSEMBLE   BRASS ENSEMBLE   WOODWIND ENSEMBLE

5

WOMEN'S VOICES   MEN'S VOICES   COMBINATION

6

WOMEN'S VOICES   MEN'S VOICES   COMBINATION

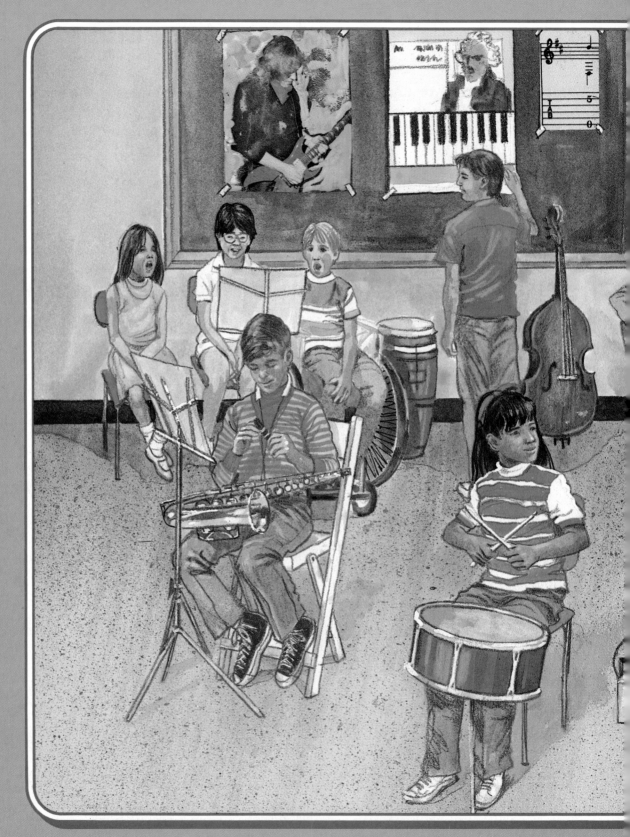

Sharing Music

Singing in Unison

This song is a musical tribute to Amelia Earhart, who is sometimes referred to as the First Lady of the Air.

As you listen to the recording, pay particular attention to the unison singing. Notice how all the voices blend together to sound like one voice.

Lady of the Air

Words and Music by John Carter and Mary Kay Beall

La - dy ___ of the air, my A - me - lia,

La - dy ___ of the air, my i - deal,

La - dy won't you say where you are to - day?

La - dy of the air, A - me - lia. ___

A

Lady ___ of the air, my A - me - lia,

Lady ___ of the air, my i - deal,

Lady won't you say where you are to - day?

(last time to Coda)

Lady of the air, A - me ___ lia.

B

1. Once in a life - time a la - dy does what no
2. Once in a life - time a la - dy flies o - ver

oth - er can do; ___
land ___ and sea; ___

O - pen the eyes ___ of the
Dar - ing to go ___ where ___

world to see that la - dies can make dreams come true! Oh,
ev' - ry one knows dan - ger is cer - tain to be. Oh

D.C.

Coda

A - me - lia ___

Two Ways to Create Harmony

The Water Is Wide

(Version One)

Folk Song from England

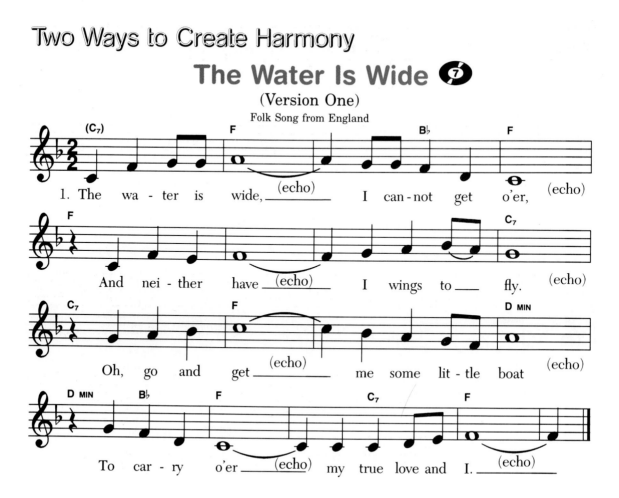

1. The wa-ter is wide, (echo) I can-not get o'er, (echo)
And nei-ther have (echo) I wings to fly. (echo)
Oh, go and get (echo) me some lit-tle boat (echo)
To car-ry o'er (echo) my true love and I. (echo)

2. There is a ship sailing on the sea,
   She's loaded deep as deep can be,
   But not so deep as in love I am;
   I care not if I sink or swim.

3. Oh, love is handsome and love is fine,
   And love is charming when it is true,
   As it grows older it grows cold
   And fades away like morning dew.

The Water Is Wide

(Version Two)

Folk Song from England

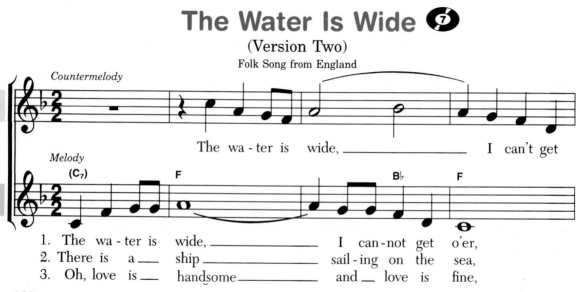

Countermelody

The wa-ter is wide, I can't get

Melody

1. The wa-ter is wide, I can-not get o'er,
2. There is a ship sail-ing on the sea,
3. Oh, love is handsome and love is fine,

How is harmony created in version one of "The Water Is Wide"?
How is harmony created in version two?

Echoing the Melody

Let's Go Singin' ⑦

Words and Music by Dianne Baker

Let's go sing-in' ___ down that road. _____

Let's go sing-in' ___ down that road. _

___ Let's go sing - in' ___ where ev-er we go. ___

___ Let's go sing - in'; ___ sing-in' ev-'ry where we

This road is rock-y _____ life's not ea-sy ___ this ___ we

go, This road is rock-y _____ life's not ea-sy ___ this ___ we

know, So we'll go sing-in' ___ where ev-er we go. ___

know, So we'll go sing-in' where ev-er we go. ___

1. We'll look to the fu - ture __ and live each day as it __ ap-pears
2. This road's al-ways wind - ing __ through hills and val-leys of __ our mind.

Each sun - rise, oh, so pre-cious, with its hopes and fears, ____
Dark clouds go drift-in' ov - er, may be sil - ver lined. ____

We're in this to-geth - er __ The time is not so long; _____
We'll not be dis-cour - aged _ We'll see the sun be-fore too long.

We'll make the most of what _ we __ have, Sing-in' a song. ____
We'll make the most of what _ we __ have, Sing-in' a song. ____

Parts for Percussion

Here are four percussion parts to play during section A.
Which one will you try?

Adding Countermelodies

The title "Oh, Be Joyful" tells you how this song should be sung.

Oh, Be Joyful

From Gaudeamus Hodie   Words and Music by Natalie Sleeth

1. Oh, be joy-ful, Oh, be ju - bi-lant, Put your sor-rows far a - way, _
2. We will sing a song of friend - ship, We will raise our voi-ces strong, _

We re - joice and sing to - geth - er this hap - py day.
We'll re-joice and sing to - geth - er the whole day long.

Add a Countermelody

When you know the melody of "Oh, Be Joyful," try this easy
countermelody. Notice how the tones move in the first six
measures.

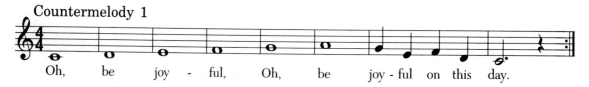

Oh, be joy - ful, Oh, be joy - ful on this day.

Here is another countermelody to add to a performance of
"Oh, Be Joyful."

Oh, be joy - ful, Oh, be joy - ful,

Oh, be joy - ful, put your sor - rows a - way.

Bells and Recorders

Team up with two friends and try playing this arrangement of "Oh, Be Joyful," using bells or recorders.

Layers of Countermelodies

As you listen to this lively song, pay particular attention to how the tones move at the end of the second line.

Sing along with the voices on the recording when you can.

Chumbara 8

French-Canadian Folk Song

1. Chum-ba-ra, _____ chum-ba-ra chum-ba-ra, _____ chum-ba-ra

chum-ba-ra, _____ chum-ba-ra chum, chum, chum, chum, chum, chum, chum, chum,

Chum-ba-ra, _____ chum-ba-ra chum-ba-ra, _____ chum-ba-ra

chum-ba-ra, _____ chum-ba-ra chum, chum, chum!

2. Fy-do-lee

3. Chow-ber-ski

4. Chug-ah-lee

5. Say-too-mee

6. Boom-ta-da

7. Zow-lee-ski

Four Countermelodies

You can build layers of sound by adding these countermelodies one at a time.

Countermelody 1

Chum chum chum chum, Chum chum chum chum, Chum chum chum chum, Chum!

Countermelody 2

Doo-bee doo-bee doo,   Doo-bee doo-bee doo,

Doo-bee doo-bee doo,   Doo-bee doo-bee doo.

Countermelody 3

Bah dah bah dah dah, Bah dah bah dah dah,

Bah dah bah dah dah, Dah.

Countermelody 4

Noh   noh noh noh,   Noh   noh noh noh,

Noh noh noh noh noh, Noh noh noh noh.

Listen for the descending scale passage in this sprightly music by Jacques Offenbach.

"Cancan" from *Gaité Parisienne*........Offenbach

Dynamics and Performance

Bless the Beasts and Children

(From the Columbia Pictures Release: "Bless the Beasts and Children")
Words and Music by Barry de Vorzon and Perry Botkin, Jr.   Arranged by Sol Berkowitz

177

Performance in Gospel Style

As you listen to "Down by the Riverside," keep time to the music with this tap-snap pattern.

(tap   snap   tap   snap)

Down by the Riverside

Black Spiritual

1. Gon - na   lay   down   my   sword and   shield __
2. Gon - na   join   hands   with   ev' - ry   one, __
3. Gon - na   ring   out   a   song   of   joy, __

Down   by   the   riv - er - side, __

Down   by   the   riv - er - side, __

Down   by   the   riv - er - side, __

Gon - na   lay   down   my   sword and   shield, __
Gon - na   join   hands   with   ev' - ry   one, __
Gon - na   ring   out   a   song   of   joy, __

178

Down by the riv - er - side, ___

And stud - y ___ war no more. ___

B
I ain't gon - na stud - y ___ war no more,

I ain't gon - na stud - y ___ war no more,

I ain't gon - na stud - y ___ war no

1. more. ___ I ain't gon - na

2. more. ___

Accompaniment Patterns

Use these patterns to accompany the singing.

Autoharp strum

Tambourine

Words and Music

"Suliram" *(Soo-lee-rahm)* is an Indonesian lullaby. Before you listen to the recording, decide how you think this song should be sung. Can you think of adjectives that might describe the mood that is suggested by the words?

Suliram

Indonesian Folk Song   Words by Marc Merson

Su - li - ram, Su - li - ram, ram, ram.

comes far a - way, Su - li - ram."

But shad - ows fly off be - yond the farth - est sea, ___

D.S. al Fine

And when you wak - en, you'll still be here with me. ___ Su - li -

On this recording you will hear some instrumental music from Indonesia. It is played by a Javanese gamelan, an ensemble of metallophones and bronze gongs of different shapes and sizes.

Bubaran: Golden Rain . . . Javanese Court Gamelan

Percussion Accompaniments

When you can feel the steady beat in this song, play a
tambourine pattern in time to the music.

Tumba

Palestinian Melody

I

Tum - ba tum - ba tum - ba tum, Tum - ba tum - ba tum - ba tum.

II

La la la la la la, La la la la la,

La la la la la la, La la la la.

III

Tum - ba, Tum - ba, Tum - ba.

The editors of Silver Burdett Company have made every attempt to verify the source of "Tumba," but were unable to do so. We believe the song to be
in the public domain.

Bell Patterns

Choose one of these bell patterns to play as an
accompaniment for "Tumba."

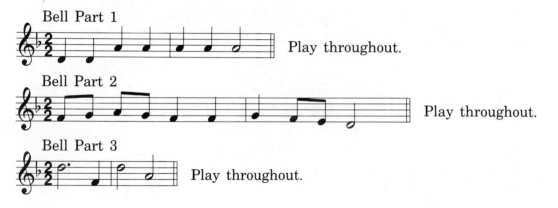

Bell Part 1

Play throughout.

Bell Part 2

Play throughout.

Bell Part 3

Play throughout.

Orff Instrument Arrangement

A Three-Part Round

When "Gloria in Excelsis Deo"
is sung as a round, it should
sound like a peal of bells.
Listen to the recording and try
to identify the instrument that
accompanies the song.

Gloria in Excelsis Deo

Music by Christopher Le Fleming

Belwin Mills Music Ltd. Used by permission.

Can you identify the instrument that plays this piece?

A Song for Bells . . . . Pinkham

184

A Four-Part Round

Listen to the recording of "Glory to God in the Highest." What happens to the sound of the music as different parts are added to the performance?

Glory to God in the Highest

Music by Christopher Le Fleming

Belwin-Mills Music Ltd. Used by permission.

Here is a bell ostinato to play as others sing the song.

Bell ostinato

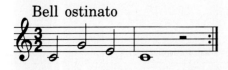

Thin Sound–Thick Sound

Different musical textures can be created, using the song and bell ostinato. For example, follow this performance routine.

- Sing the song.
- Sing the song with bell accompaniment.
- Sing the song as a round.
- Sing the song as a round with bell accompaniment.

An American Composer

The music you will hear is from Leonard Bernstein's *Mass*—a theater piece for singers, players, and dancers. Bernstein created the work for the opening of the John F. Kennedy Center for the Performing Arts in Washington, D.C.

As you listen to the recording, think about what is going on in the music. What do you hear?

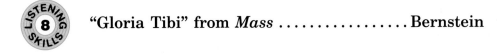

LISTENING SKILLS 8   "Gloria Tibi" from *Mass* . . . . Bernstein

An Unusual Meter

One of the qualities that makes Bernstein's "Gloria Tibi" so exciting is the strong, driving rhythm that is heard and felt from the beginning of the piece to the very end.

Look at the rhythm pattern notated below. What does the meter signature tell you? Try tapping or clapping the pattern along with the bongo part as you listen to "Gloria Tibi" again.

Leonard Bernstein was born in Lawrence, Massachusetts. He attended Harvard University and the Curtis Institute of music. He continued his musical education at Tanglewood (home of the Berkshire Music Festival) during the summers of 1940–1943. When Bernstein was a young man of 25, he was appointed assistant conductor of the New York Philharmonic. He became famous overnight when he filled in for a conductor who was suddenly taken ill. In 1958, Bernstein became the first American-born conductor to be appointed director of the New York Philharmonic—one of the greatest orchestras in the world.

Leonard Bernstein
(1918–   )

Adding Ostinatos

In order to sing "Spring Song" as a four-part round, you must be able to do two things well:

• Sing the melody independently. • Keep the beat steady.

Spring Song

Words and Music by John Horman

When _ in the spring the warm winds _ blow, And _

life be - gins _ a - new, Let us lift our voi - ces

to the _ sky and _ bring this song to you.

This is spring! This is spring! Win - ter's gone and far be - hind

are the wind and the rain and the snow up - on the pine.

Text and Melody by John Horman

Add a Part

All three of these ostinatos can be added to a performance of "Spring Song." Which one will you play?

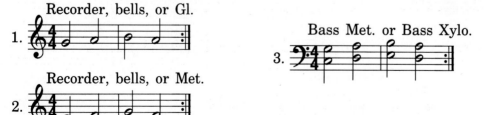

Recorder, bells, or Gl.

1.

Recorder, bells, or Met.

2.

Bass Met. or Bass Xylo.

3.

188

Introductions and Codas

When your class knows the melody of "Old Abram Brown,"
sing the song as a two-, three-, or four-part round.

Old Abram Brown

Benjamin Britten

Words from "Tom Tiddler's Ground" by Walter de la Mare. Copyright 1936 by Boosey & Co., Ltd.; Renewed 1963. Reprinted by permission of Boosey & Hawkes, Inc.

Using the bells or a recorder, play one of these parts as an
introduction to the song. Play a different part as a coda, to
end the performance.

Tempo and Performance

Composers often write Italian words in their music, to tell the performers how fast or how slow to sing. You will find four words that indicate tempo in the score of "Let There Be Peace on Earth." Each word is shown in a color box. Listen to the recording, then tell what you think each word means.

Let There Be Peace on Earth

Words and Music by Sy Miller and Jill Jackson

Let there be peace on earth, And let it be-gin with me. _____

Let there be peace on earth, The peace that was meant to be. _____

With God as our Fa-ther, _____ Broth-ers all are we. _____

Let me walk with my broth-er _____ in per-fect har-mo-ny. _____

Let peace be-gin with me, Let this be the mo-ment now: _____

With ev-'ry step I take, Let this be my sol-emn vow: _____

To take each mo-ment and live each mo-ment In peace e-ter-nal - ly, _____

To take each mo-ment and live each mo-ment In peace e-ter-nal - ly, _____

Let there be peace on earth And let it be - gin _ with me. _____

Let there be peace on earth And let it be - gin _ with me. _____

PEACEABLE KINGDOM (DETAIL)
EDWARD HICKS, 1834

Follow the Score

Follow the score of "Sunny Day" as you listen to the recording.
What signs do you find that tell you how loud or how soft to sing?

Sunny Day

Words and Music by Terre McPheeters

1. Ev - 'ry time it rains, I won - der why _____ it
2. I don't want the rain to bring me down, _____ I'd

makes me sad ____ it makes me cry, ___ But
rath - er smile _ than wear a frown, _ So

ev - 'ry time I see the sun up a - bove _____ it
come _ on _ sun _ I'm countin' on you _____ to

REFRAIN

feels like ev - 'ry one's in love. ___ Send me a
change _ the _ skies to blue. ___

sun - ny day, ___ Send me a clear blue sky, ___

Rain and clouds, Oh,

You can take all the rain ___ and the clouds a - way _ So when I

Try reading this poem aloud. How will you use your speaking
voice to help express what the words mean?

How Gray the Rain

How gray the rain
And gray the world
And gray the rain clouds overhead,
When suddenly
Some cloud is furled
And there is gleaming sun instead!

The raindrops drip
Prismatic light,
And trees and meadows burn in green,
And arched in air
Serene and bright
The rainbow all at once is seen.

Elisabeth Coatsworth

Sing and Dance

As you listen to "Evening of Roses," play the first beat in each measure, using a hand drum.

Evening of Roses

Hebrew Song by M. Dor and J. Hadar   English Words by L. M. Wiedman

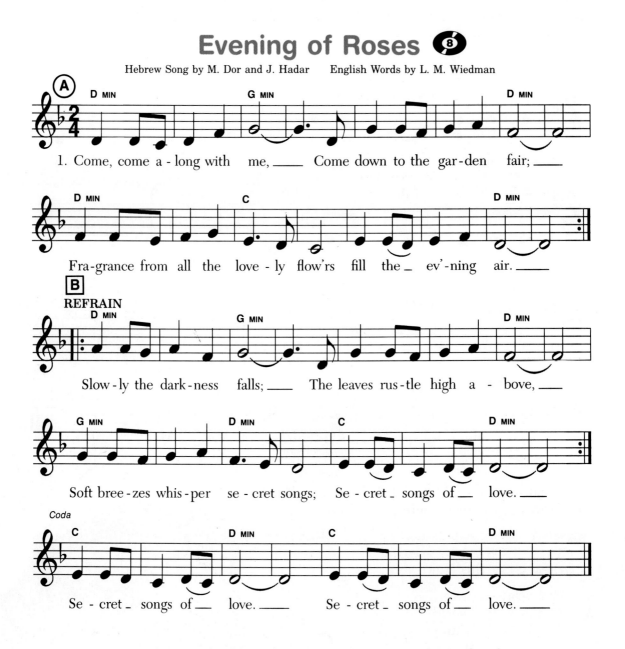

1. Come, come a - long with me, ___ Come down to the gar-den fair; ___

Fra - grance from all the love - ly flow'rs fill the _ ev' - ning air. ___

REFRAIN

Slow - ly the dark - ness falls; ___ The leaves rus - tle high a - bove, ___

Soft bree - zes whis - per se - cret songs; Se - cret _ songs of _ love. ___

Coda

Se - cret _ songs of _ love. ___ Se - cret _ songs of _ love. ___

2. Come, come along with me, Come down to the garden fair;
   There the scent of roses fill the ev'ning air. *(Repeat)*
   Refrain *(Repeat)*
   Coda

Used by Permission of ACUM, Ltd., Tel Aviv, Israel.

Move to the Music

Form a circle with your classmates, joining hands in a *V* position as shown in the illustration below.

Practice walking the steady beat (eight beats counterclockwise, then eight beats clockwise) to the music of section A. Use the following movement pattern.

♩ ♩ ♩ ♩ ♩ ♩ ♩ ♩

Walk 2 3 4; 5 6 side touch.
  R   L R L R L R L

♩ ♩ ♩ ♩ ♩ ♩ ♩ ♩

Walk 2 3 4; 5 6 side touch.
  L   R L R L R L (R)

The following lists suggest two different styles of performance. Look at the two-line lyric after each number below and decide which list best suits the style of each set of lyrics. On your worksheet, write A or B in the blank.

A	B
energetic	serene
bright	calm
cheerful	gentle
vigorous	quiet

1 _____

Silent night, holy night,
All is calm, all is bright.

2 _____

Take me out to the ball game,
Take me out with the crowd.

3 _____

Swing along the open road
Under skies so blue.

4 _____

Goodnight to you all
And sweet be your dreams.

5 _____

When at night I go to sleep,
Fourteen angels watch will keep.

6 _____

Lift ev'ry voice and sing
Till earth and heaven ring.

What Do You Hear? 9

Texture

You will hear four sets of pieces. In each set, one piece has a thin texture, the other, a thick texture. Listen to both pieces, decide which has a thin texture and which has a thick texture, then circle your answers on your worksheet.

1 First piece   THIN   THICK

   Second piece   THIN   THICK

2 First piece   THIN   THICK

   Second piece   THIN   THICK

3 First piece   THIN   THICK

   Second piece   THIN   THICK

4 First piece   THIN   THICK

   Second piece   THIN   THICK

Look in the right-hand column for the definition of each symbol or word in the left-hand column. On your worksheet, write its letter in the blank.

1 _____ *f*   **A** soft

2 _____ *moderato*   **B** gradually getting faster

3 _____ ▭   **C** moderately soft

4 _____ *p*   **D** majestic

5 _____ *ritardando*   **E** moderate

6 _____ *mp*   **F** loud

7 _____ ◁   **G** getting softer

8 _____ *mf*   **H** slowing up

9 _____ *maestoso*   **I** getting louder

10 _____ *accelerando*   **J** moderately loud

You have learned that vocal harmony can be created in a variety of ways. Listen to eight songs from your book. As you listen to each song, decide how harmony is created in the voice parts. When a number is called, listen, then circle your answer on your worksheet.

1 MELODY WITH COUNTERMELODY   ROUND   PART SONG

2 MELODY WITH COUNTERMELODY   ROUND   PART SONG

3 MELODY WITH COUNTERMELODY   ROUND   PART SONG

4 MELODY WITH COUNTERMELODY   ROUND   PART SONG

5 MELODY WITH COUNTERMELODY   ROUND   PART SONG

6 MELODY WITH COUNTERMELODY   ROUND   PART SONG

7 MELODY WITH COUNTERMELODY   ROUND   PART SONG

8 MELODY WITH COUNTERMELODY   ROUND   PART SONG

Let's Hear It for America

Words and Music by Carmino Ravosa

Chorus

1.,2.,3. Let's hear it for A - mer - i - ca, Hip, hoo - ray, Let's hear it for A - mer - i - ca, Hip, hoo - ray, Let's hear it for A - mer - i - ca, Hip, hoo - ray. _____

(Solo 1—second time) We're a coun - try that is free *(Solo 2—second time)* from sea to

(Solo 3—second time) shin - ing sea, We've ev - 'ry right to brag,

D.C. al Fine (after 2nd time)

(Solo 4—second time) And hold up high our flag. _____ *(Slower last time)* So let's

201

Student 1: What a country! I've been reading about it in this book. *(Opens book.)* Look at all these famous names. What heroes!

Student 2: He's (she's) right. Someone once said that the history of the world is but the biography of great men and women.

Student 3: The same thing can be said about the history of America. Everybody's got to have a hero. We all have one.

Ev'rybody's Got to Have a Hero

Words and Music by Carmino Ravosa

VERSE

Solo 1 1. Ev - 'ry-bod - y's got to have a he - ro,
Solo 2 2. Ev - 'ry-bod - y's got to have a he - ro,

Some - one they would real - ly like to be,
Some - one they can real - ly look up to,

Ev - 'ry-bod-y's got to have a he - ro, like me.
Ev - 'ry-bod-y's got to have a he - ro, like you.

REFRAIN
Chorus

He - roes come in man - y shapes and siz - es;

He - roes come in man - y col - ors, too.

He - roes can be male or can be fe - male,

It's what they ac - com - plish, what they do.

Ev - 'ry - bod - y's got to have a he - ro,

Some - one in their life who is a plus,

Ev - 'ry - bod - y's got to have a he - ro, like us.

Student 4: We all have our heroes—our own personal heroes who have written some of the most glorious pages in American history. We'd like to tell you about them. *(Students tell about their heroes.)*

Student 5: Hey! All these famous names you're tossing around makes me feel kind of ordinary and unimportant.

Student 6: Now wait a minute, that's not so. We may have another Amelia Earhart or Thomas Edison right here in this school—maybe in our own class!

Student 7: And Earhart and Edison didn't know they were going to be famous. When they were young they were just like me—just like you.

Just Like You 9

Words and Music by Carmino Ravosa

(Solo) VERSE

(Spoken) 1. All the peo-ple you think __ of as great or as fa - mous,
(Spoken) 2. All the peo-ple you think __ of as great or as fa - mous,

Oh, they did - n't start __ out that way. They have
They real - ly all start - ed the same. They had

some-thing in com - mon, yes, some-thing in com - mon,
some-thing in com - mon, yes, some-thing in com - mon,

No i - dea they'd be fa - mous one day.
Be - fore you ev - er heard __ of their name.

REFRAIN

(Sung) They were just like — you, — they were just like — you. —

They were lit - tle chil - dren once, it's — true,

And they did all the things that boys and girls do, —

1.

And they grew, and they grew, and they grew. ——

2.

— grew. Like you.

Student 8: You're right. I'm sure my hero—Abraham Lincoln— had no idea that he'd grow up to be president of the U.S.A. *(Students give short reports about their favorite presidents.)*

Student 9: Do you realize that any one of us can grow up to be president?

You Can Grow Up to Be President

Words and Music by Carmino Ravosa

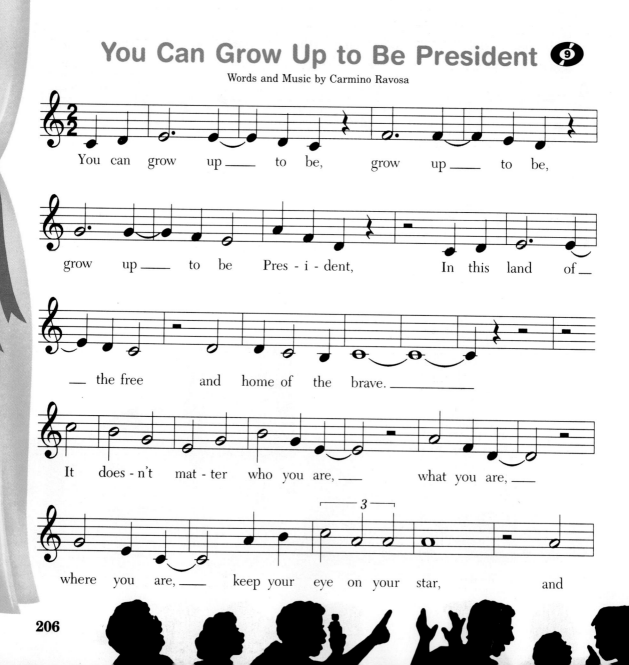

You can grow up ___ to be, grow up ___ to be,

grow up ___ to be Pres - i - dent, In this land of ___

___ the free and home of the brave. _____

It does - n't mat - ter who you are, ___ what you are, ___

where you are, ___ keep your eye on your star, and

Student 10: You've all been talking about heroes that are *famous* men and women. But you've never even heard about *my* heroes. They're my ancestors!

All: Ancestors?

Student 11: I never thought of that—ancestors *are* heroes. Just think of those early settlers who came to our shores so long ago.

Student 12: Some came seeking religious freedom.

Student 13: Some came to escape political tyranny.

Student 14: Some came hoping to make a better life for themselves and their families.

Student 15: And those early settlers were very brave. Why some of them came across the water with only a few precious possessions and the clothes on their back.

All of Us

Words and Music by Carmino Ravosa

1.–2. All of us come a - cross the wa - ter, _____

All of us come a - cross the sea, _____

All of us come from some - where, _____

You're no dif - f'rent than me. _____

2.,3.,4.,5.

From the old coun - try.

Coda

All of us come a - cross the wa - ter.

3. Some of us, we were born in Ireland,
   England, Germany,
   India, Africa, Asia,
   Russia, Italy.

4. Some of us come from Puerto Rico,
   Poland, Sweden, France,
   China, and Japan.
   We too want a chance.

5. All of us come across the water,
   All of us come across to be
   In this golden land of plenty
   And opportunity. (To coda)

Student 16: What courage those people had! They cleared the land and built their homes.

Student 17: They tilled the soil and planted crops.

Student 18: They laid the railroad tracks and dug canals.

Student 19: And my ancestors crossed the country in covered wagons and settled in the West. They thought it was the finest land they ever did see.

Finest Land

Words and Music by Carmino Ravosa

REFRAIN

Fin-est land you ev - er did see, Fin-est land in the whole coun-try,

Fin-est land you ev - er did see, Fin-est land and it's all free! All free!

1. Corn grows high e - nough to hang your hat,
2. Wheat grows high e - nough to touch the sky,
3. Land so rich __ that you hear folks say,

Corn grows high e - nough to hang your hat,
Wheat grows high e - nough to touch the sky,
Land so rich __ that you hear folks say,

Ears grow just a-bout as big as that,
Would I fib to you or tell a lie!
"What you plant — you can eat that day,

D.C. al Fine (after 3rd verse)

Ears grow just a-bout as big as that.
Would I fib to you or tell a lie!
What you plant — you can eat that day."

Student 20: Walt Whitman, a famous American poet, once said that the dollar-a-day factory hands, the humble pioneer farmers, and the corner shopkeepers were the *true* heroes of our country in those early days.

Student 21: So you see, it's not only the powerful and the privileged—the Washingtons and the Lincolns—who are heroes. More often it's just ordinary people working together who shape a nation and help to make it great.

You Are What Makes America Great ⑨

Words and Music by Carmino Ravosa

1. You   are what makes   A - mer - i - ca great,
2. You   are what makes   A - mer - i - ca strong,

You   are her fu - ture,   You   are her fate;
You   are her mor - als, her   hope   and her song;

You are what makes A - mer - i - ca great. _____ strong. _____

You may not make the head - lines, not man - y peo - ple do,

And you may not be quot - ed or be in a "Who's Who,"

But still you are im - por - tant, and if you real - ly care,

rit.

You can let the world know that you are there.

Slower

You are what makes A - mer - i - ca grow,

You are her mus - cles, her get up and go,

rit.

You are what makes A - mer - i - ca grow. _____

Student 22: We've enjoyed doing this show for you and sharing some of our thoughts about this country we live in. We all have an opportunity to write the next chapter in the American story. And what better way to start than to say something *good* about America.

Say Something Good About America

Words and Music by Carmino Ravosa

REFRAIN

Say some-thing good a-bout A - mer - i - ca, A - mer - i - ca, A - mer - i - ca, Say some-thing good a-bout A - mer - i - ca, A - mer - i - ca to - day.

Fine

VERSE

1. We've got a lot to be proud of,
2. No - bod - y said we were per - fect,

We've got a lot we can cheer, _____
We've got our faults you can see, _____

We've ev - 'ry right to be thank - ful, _____
But we've got some - thing to build on, _____

D.C. al Fine (after 2nd verse)

That in this world we are here. _____
That we're a coun - try that's free. _____

Jan	1 2 3 4 5 6	Jul	1 2 3 **4** 6
	7 8 9 10 11 12 13 14 15		7 8 9 10 11 12 13 14 15
	16 17 18 19 20 21 22 23 24		16 17 18 19 20 21 22 23 24
	25 26 27 28 29 30 31		25 26 27 28 29 30 31
Feb	1 2 3 4 5 6	Aug	1 2 3 4 5 6
	7 8 9 10 11 12 13 14 15		7 8 9 10 11 12 13 14 15
	16 17 18 19 20 21 22 23 24		16 17 18 19 20 21 22 23 24
	25 26 27 28		25 26 27 28 29 30 31
Mar	1 2 3 4 5 6	Sep	1 2 3 4 5 6
	7 8 9 10 11 12 13 14 15		7 8 9 10 11 12 13 14 15
	16 17 18 19 20 21 22 23 24		16 17 18 19 20 21 22 23 24
	25 26 27 28 29 30 31		25 26 27 28 29 30
Apr	1 2 3 4 5 6	Oct	1 2 3 4 5 6
	7 8 9 10 11 12 13 14 15		7 8 9 10 11 12 13 14 15
	16 17 18 19 20 21 22 23 24		16 17 18 19 20 21 22 23 24
	25 26 27 28 29 30		25 26 27 28 29 30 31
May	1 2 3 4 5 6	Nov	1 2 3 4 5 6
	7 8 9 10 11 12 13 14 15		7 8 9 10 11 12 13 14 15
	16 17 18 19 20 21 22 23 24		16 17 18 19 20 21 22 23 24
	25 26 27 28 29 30		25 26 27 28 29 30
Jun	1 2 3 4 5 6	Dec	1 2 3 4 5 6
	7 8 9 10 11 12 13 14 15		7 8 9 10 11 12 13 14 15
	16 17 18 19 20 21 22 23 24		16 17 18 19 20 21 22 23 24
	25 26 27 28 29 30		25 26 27 28 29 30 31

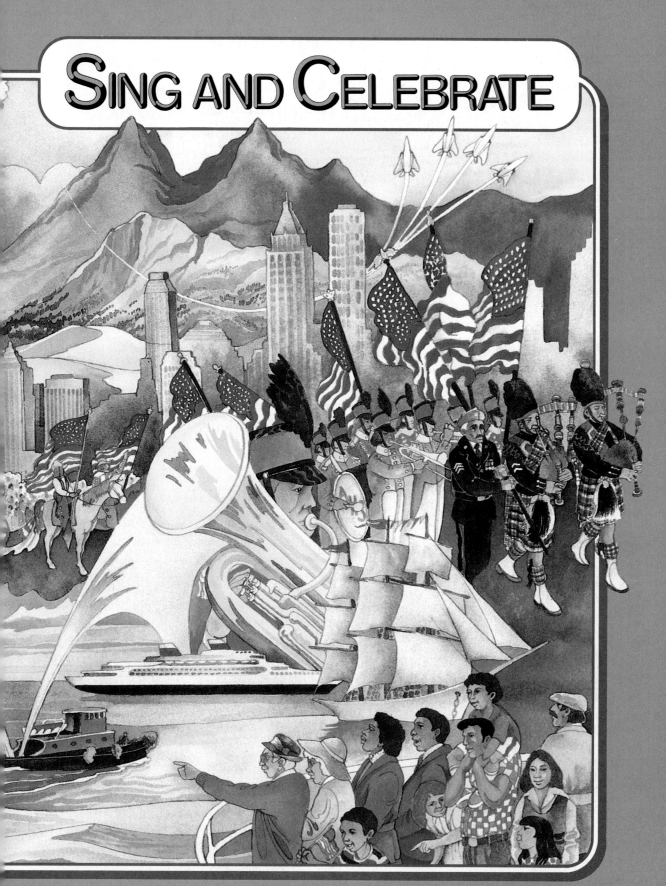

SING AND CELEBRATE

Our National Anthem

During the War of 1812, Francis Scott Key wrote the words of this song after spending an anxious night awaiting the outcome of an enemy bombardment at Fort McHenry. However, it was not until 1931 that an act of Congress established "The Star-Spangled Banner" as the national anthem of the United States.

The Star-Spangled Banner

Music by John Stafford Smith   Words by Francis Scott Key

1. Oh, __ say! can you see, by the dawn's ear - ly light, What so
2. On the shore, dim - ly seen through the mists of the deep, Where the

proud - ly we hailed at the twi-light's last gleam-ing, Whose broad
foe's haugh-ty host in dread si - lence re - pos - es, What is

stripes and bright stars, through the per - il - ous fight, O'er the
that which the breeze, o'er the tow - er - ing steep, As it

ram - parts we watched were so gal - lant - ly stream - ing? And the
fit - ful - ly blows, half con - ceals, half dis - clos - es? Now it

rock - ets' red glare, the bombs burst - ing in air, Gave
catch - es the gleam of the morn - ing's first beam, In full

proof through the night that our flag was still there. Oh,
glo - ry re - flected now — shines on the stream; 'Tis the

say, does that — Star-Span-gled Ban - ner — yet — wave — O'er the
Star-Span - gled — Ban - ner, oh, long may — it — wave — O'er the

land — of the free and the home of the brave?
land — of the free and the home of the brave!

3. Oh, thus be it ever when free men shall stand
   Between their loved homes and the war's desolation!
   Blest with vict'ry and peace, may the heav'n-rescued land
   Praise the Pow'r that hath made and preserved us a nation!
   Then conquer we must, for our cause it is just,
   And this be our motto: "In God is our trust!"
   And the Star-Spangled Banner in triumph shall wave
   O'er the land of the free and the home of the brave!

Sweet Freedom's Song

Samuel Francis Smith was inspired to write the words of this
well-known patriotic hymn while he was still a young student.
A group of school children gave the first performance of
"America" in Boston, Massachusetts, on July 4, 1832.

America 9

Traditional Melody   Words by Samuel Francis Smith

1. My coun - try! 'tis of thee, Sweet land of
2. My na - tive coun - try, thee, Land of the

lib - er - ty, Of thee I sing; Land where my
no - ble free, Thy name I love; I love thy

fa - thers died, Land of the Pil - grims' pride,
rocks and rills, Thy woods and tem - pled hills,

From ev - 'ry moun - tain - side Let free - dom ring!
My heart with rap - ture thrills Like that a - bove.

3. Let music swell the breeze, And ring from all the trees
   Sweet Freedom's song;
   Let mortal tongues awake, Let all that breathe partake,
   Let rocks their silence break, The sound prolong.

4. Our fathers' God, to Thee, Author of liberty,
   To Thee we sing;
   Long may our land be bright With Freedom's holy light;
   Protect us by Thy might, Great God, our King!

A View of America

On a beautiful day in 1893, Katharine Lee Bates stood on the top of Colorado's Pikes Peak and looked for miles in every direction. She seemed to be seeing all of America—mountains, valleys, wide prairies. It was after this experience that she wrote the poem "America, the Beautiful."

America, the Beautiful 9

Words by Katharine Lee Bates   Music by Samuel A. Ward

1. O beau - ti - ful for spa - cious skies, For am - ber waves of grain,
For pur - ple moun - tain maj - es - ties A - bove the fruit - ed plain!
A - mer - i - ca! A - mer - i - ca! God shed His grace on thee
And crown thy good with broth - er - hood, From sea to shin - ing sea!

2. O beautiful for Pilgrim feet, Whose stern impassioned stress
   A thoroughfare for freedom beat Across the wilderness!
   America! America! God mend thine ev'ry flaw,
   Confirm thy soul in self control, Thy liberty in law!

3. O beautiful for patriot dream That sees, beyond the years,
   Thine alabaster cities gleam, Undimmed by human tears!
   America! America! God shed His grace on thee,
   And crown thy good with brotherhood, From sea to shining sea!

Sing for America

Play a drum beat on your knees as you listen to this music.

I Like It Here

Words and Music by Clay Boland

I like the U - nit - ed States of A - mer - i - ca, _____
I am so luck - y to be in A - mer - i - ca, _____

I like the way we all live with - out fear; _____
And I am thank - ful each day of the year, _____

I like to vote for my choice, ___ speak my mind, raise my voice,
For I can do as I please, ___ 'cause I'm free as the breeze,

1. Yes, I like it here. _____
2. like it here. _____

I'd like to climb to the top of a moun - tain so high, ___

Lift my head to the sky ___ and say how grate - ful am I _____

For the way that I'm liv - ing, I'm work - ing and giv - ing

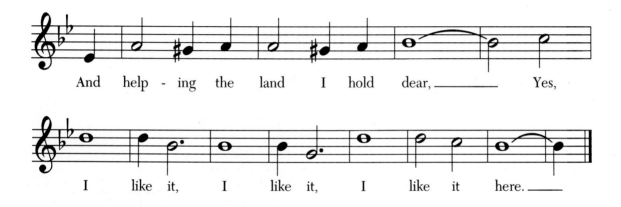

And help - ing the land I hold dear, _____ Yes,

I like it, I like it, I like it here. _____

In this poem a great American poet praises the many voices of America—each one singing his or her own song.

I Hear America Singing

I hear America singing, the varied carols I hear,
Those of the mechanics, each singing his as it should be blithe and
    strong,
The carpenter singing his as he measures his plank or beam,
The mason singing his as he makes ready for work or leaves off
    work,
The boatman singing what belongs to him in his boat, the deck
    hand singing on the steamboat deck,
The shoemaker singing as he sits on his bench, the hatter singing
    as he stands,
The wood-cutter's song, the ploughboy's on his way in the morning,
    or at noon intermission or at sundown,
The delicious singing of the mother, or the young wife at work, or
    the girl sewing or washing,
Each sings what belongs to him or her and to none else,
The day what belongs to the day—at night the party of young
    fellows, robust, friendly,
Singing with open mouths their strong melodious songs.

Walt Whitman

Improvise a Drum Part

Make up (improvise) a drum part
as you sing the refrain of
this stirring song.

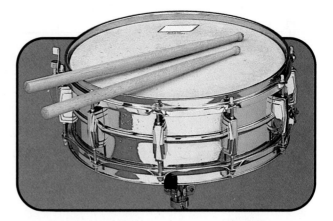

Battle Hymn of the Republic 🄈

Music by William Steffe   Words by Julia Ward Howe

1. Mine _____ eyes have seen the glo - ry of the
2. He has sound - ed forth the trum - pet that shall

com - ing of the Lord; He is tramp - ling out the vin - tage
nev - er call re - treat; He is sift - ing out the hearts of

where the grapes of wrath are stored; He hath
men be - fore the judg - ment seat. Oh, be

loosed the fate - ful light - ning of His ter - ri - ble swift sword;
swift, my soul, to an - swer Him! Be ju - bi - lant, my feet!

His truth is march - ing on.
Our God is march - ing on.

REFRAIN

Sing Out for Liberty

The words of this stirring song were written by the poet
James Weldon Johnson to commemorate the birthday of
Abraham Lincoln. The words were set to music by
J. Rosamond Johnson, the poet's brother.

Lift Ev'ry Voice and Sing ⑨

Words by James Weldon Johnson   Music by Rosamond Johnson

1. Lift ev'-ry voice and sing, till earth and heav-en ring,
2. Ston-y the road we trod, bit-ter the chas-t'ning rod

Ring with the har-mo-nies of lib-er-ty.
Felt in the days when hope un-born had died.

Let our re-joic-ing rise, high as the lis-t'ning skies,
Yet with a stead-y beat, have not our wea-ry feet

Let it re-sound loud as the roll-ing sea.
Come to the place for which our fa-thers died.

Sing a song full of the faith that the dark past has taught us;
We have come o-ver a way that with tears has been wa-tered;

Sing a song full of the hope that the pres-ent has brought us;
We have come tread-ing our path through the blood of the slaugh - tered;

Fac-ing the ris - ing sun of our new day be - gun,
Out from the gloom - y past, till now we stand at _____ last

Let us march on till vic - to - ry _____ is won.
Where the white gleam of our bright star _____ is cast.

Dear Land of All My Love

Long as thine Art shall love true love,
Long as thy Science truth shall know,
Long as thine Eagle harms no Dove,
Long as thy Law by law shall grow,
Long as thy God is God above,
Thy brother every man below,
So long, dear Land of all my love,
Thy name shall shine, thy fame shall glow!

Sidney Lanier

Halloween Dances

In this song a number of make-believe characters dance on Halloween night. The title of the song tells you about one dance. How many other dances can you identify? Follow the words as you listen to the recording.

When Witches Were Waltzing

Words and Music by Linda Williams

1. One night I went walk-ing out in-to the wood, And
2. I want-ed to watch, so I hid in a tree. I
3. They waltzed in the wood by the light of the stars. The

found I had wan-dered much more than I should, For I came to a
said to my-self, "Can't be-lieve what I see!" It's a pump-kin
scare-crows were strum-ming their ghost-ly gui-

1. and 2.

mea-dow, a mag-i-cal spot, Where witch-es were waltz-ing. I nev-er for-
polk-a, a gob-lin ga-votte, and witch-es were waltz-ing. I nev-er for-

got what a wild and weird and won-der-ful sight, When witch-es were

waltz - ing ... on Hal - lo-ween night! ... -tars for the

skel - e - ton sam - ba, the mon - ster min - u - et, the pump - kin
witch - es were

pol - ka, the gob - lin ga - votte; And
waltz - ing, I nev - er for - got What a

wild and weird and won - der - ful sight When witch - es were

waltz - ing ... on Hal - lo-ween night.

4. One day I'll wake up in a wandering mood;
   The West wind will whisper, "Away to the wood!"
   And if you will go with me, we might take a chance;
   We'll dress all in black and we'll join in the dance!
   And we'll all rock and roll while the jack-o-lanterns jitterbug,
   The skeletons samba, the monsters minuet,
   The pumpkins polka, the goblins gavotte.
   I've been there before and I never forgot
   What a wild . . .

Listen for the "skeleton dancers" in this piece for orchestra.

Danse Macabre . . . . **Saint-Saëns**

A Song for All Nations

We celebrate United Nations Day on October 24. Why would this song be a good one to sing on that day?

We Come to Greet You in Peace
(Hevenu Shalom Aleichem)

Hebrew Folk Song

We come to greet you in peace, ___ We come to
He - ve - nu sha - lom a - lei - chem, He - ve - nu

greet you in peace, ___ We come to greet ___ you in
sha - lom a - lei - chem, He - ve - nu sha - lom a -

peace, ___ We come to greet you, greet you,
lei - chem, He - ve - nu sha - lom, sha - lom,

1. greet ___ you in peace. We come to
sha - lom a - lei - chem. He - ve - nu

2. greet ___ you in peace.
sha - lom a - lei - chem.

A Harvest Hymn

Come, Ye Thankful People, Come

Henry Alford   George J. Elvey

1. Come, ye thank - ful peo - ple, come, Raise the song of
2. All the bless - ings of the field, All the stores the

har - vest home; All is safe - ly gath - ered in Ere the
gar - dens yield; All the fruits in full sup - ply, Rip - ened

win - ter storms be - gin; God, our Mak - er, doth pro - vide
'neath the sum - mer sky; All that spring with boun - teous hand

For our wants to be sup - plied; Come to God's own
Scat - ters o'er the smil - ing land; All that lib - 'ral

tem - ple, come, Raise the song of har - vest home.
au - tumn pours From her rich o'er - flow - ing stores.

An Old Winter Song

Listen especially for the descant in this arrangement of "Jingle Bells." It adds to the fun when singing this familiar winter song.

Jingle Bells

Words and Music by James Pierpont   Descant by E. Challis

A Song for Chanukah

Improvise a tambourine part as you listen to this song. Will you tap the instrument, shake it, or will your pattern include both tapping and shaking?

Festival of Lights

Words and Music by David Eddleman

1. Come and cel - e - brate the Fes - ti - val of Lights,
2. Come and cel - e - brate the mir - a - cle of old,

See the can - dle burn - ing, burn - ing oh, so bright;
Sing a song to praise a peo - ple brave and bold,

See the drey - dl spin - ning, spin - ning out of sight,
Sing a mir - a - cle, the sto - ry that is told,

Sing to cel - e - brate these hap - py ho - ly nights
Bright me - no - rah glow - ing, won - drous to be - hold.

Once there was a lamp a - light with oil e - nough for but one night;
Praise the Mac - ca - be - an name, who saved his land from grief and shame;

Then came the mir - a - cle: for eight full days it burned so bright.
Praise for his vic - to - ry, and lib - er - ty for all pro - claim.

234

The Feast of Lights

Chanukah, or the Feast of Lights, is one of the celebrations in the long season of midwinter holidays. People of the Jewish faith celebrate the Feast of Lights for eight days during the month of December.

The menorah (special candelabra) symbolizes the Feast of Lights. During the eight-day festival, one candle is lighted each day from an extra candle called the *shammash* (watchman).

Rock of Ages

Traditional Hebrew Melody   English Words by G. Gottheil

1 Rock of A - ges, let our song Praise Thy sav - ing pow - er;

2 Rock of A - ges, Praise Thy sav - ing pow - er;

1 Thou, a-midst the rag - ing foes, Wast our shel-t'ring tow - er.

2 Thou 'midst rag-ing foes, Our shel-t'ring tow - er.

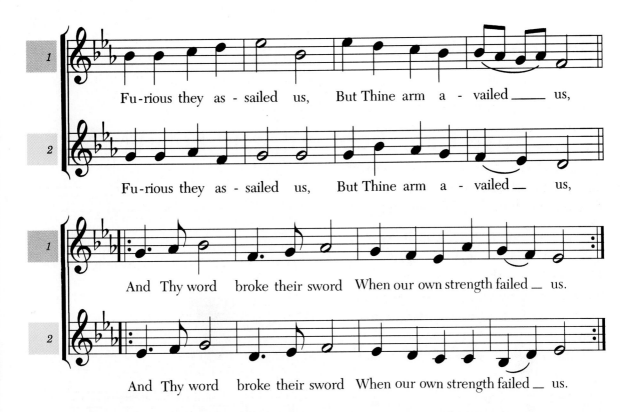

1 Fu-rious they as - sailed us, But Thine arm a - vailed _____ us,

2 Fu-rious they as - sailed us, But Thine arm a - vailed ___ us,

1 And Thy word broke their sword When our own strength failed _ us.

2 And Thy word broke their sword When our own strength failed _ us.

A Song of Always

The temple is clean,
  The lamp burns bright;
Judiah the leader,
  Has started the light.

The sun shines by days,
  And dark is the night;
But always and always
  The lamp burns bright.

Efraim Rosenzweig

A Christmas Spiritual

Do a pat toes-clap hands pattern as you listen to this song.
Join in on the chorus parts when you can.

Rise Up, Shepherd, and Follow

Black Spiritual

A Song in Two Sections

When you listen to this song, notice the contrast between the two sections. Add a stamp-clap pattern as an accompaniment in section B.

Go, Tell It on the Mountain

A VERSE
Freely

Black Spiritual

1. When I was a seek-er, I sought both night and day.
2. He made me a watch-man Up-on the cit-y wall.
3. In the time of Da-vid, Some said he was a king.

I asked the Lord to help me, And He shows me the way. ___
And if I serve Him tru-ly, I am the least of all. ___
And if a child is true born, The Lord will hear him sing. ___

B REFRAIN *(in rhythm)*

1. Go, tell it on the moun-tain, O-ver _ the hills and ev-'ry-where.

Countermelody

2. Go, tell it on the moun-tain,

1. Go, tell it on the moun-tain, Our heav'n-ly Lord _ is born.

2. Go, tell it on the moun-tain, our Lord is born.

239

An Old English Custom

The boar's head has held the place of honor at many an English Christmas dinner since the reign of Henry VIII. There is a great ceremony of bringing in the boar's head, and as part of the merriment, the "Boar's Head Carol" is sung.

Boar's Head Carol

Old English Carol

1. The boar's head in hand bear I, Be - decked with bays and rose - mar - y, And I pray you, my mas - ters be mer - ry, Quot es - tis in con - vi - vi - o.

REFRAIN

Ca - put a - pri de - fe - ro, Red - dens lau - des Do - mi - no.

2. The boar's head, I understand,
   Is the rarest dish in all the land.
   Which thus bedecked with a garland,
   Let us *servire cantico. (Refrain)*

3. Our steward hath provided this
   In honor of the King of bliss,
   Which on this day now served is,
   In Reginensi atrio. (Refrain)

241

An Old French Carol

This old French carol is known as the "Westminster Carol" in
England, probably because the choir of Westminster Abbey
was the first to sing it in that country.

Angels We Have Heard on High

Traditional French Carol

1. An - gels we have heard on high, Sweet - ly sing - ing o'er the plains,
2. Shep - herds why this ju - bi - lee? Why your joy - ous songs pro - long?

And the moun - tains in re - ply Ech - o - ing their joy - ous strains.
What the glad - some tid - ings be Which in - spire your heav'n - ly song?

REFRAIN

Glo - - - - - - - - - - - - - - - - ri - a

in ex - cel - sis De - o, Glo - - - - - - - - - - -

- - - - - - - - ri - a in ex - cel - sis De - o.

Carol from Canada

"The Huron Carol" is the first Canadian Christmas carol.
Some people believe it is the first carol of the New World.

The Huron Carol

Christmas Carol from Canada   English Words by J. E. Middleton

1. 'Twas in the moon of win-ter-time When all the birds had fled,
2. With-in a lodge of bro-ken bark The ten-der babe was found,

That might-y Git-chi Man-i-tou Sent an-gel choirs in-stead.
A rag-ged robe of rab-bit skin En-wrapped his beau-ty 'round;

Be-fore their light the stars grew dim, And won-d'ring hunt-ers heard the hymn: _
And as the hunt-er braves drew nigh The an-gel song rang loud and high: _

"Je-sus, your King, is born. Je-sus is born.

In ex-cel-sis glo-ri-a!"

3. The earliest moon of wintertime
   Is not so round and fair
   As was the ring of glory on
   The helpless infant there.
   The chiefs from far before him knelt
   With gifts of fox and beaver pelt.
   "Jesus, your King, is born.
   Jesus is born. *In excelsis gloria!*"

4. O children of the forest free,
   O sons of Manitou,
   The holy child of earth and heav'n
   Is born today for you.
   Come kneel before the radiant boy
   Who brings you beauty, peace, and joy.
   "Jesus, your King, is born.
   Jesus is born. *In excelsis gloria!*"

Three King's Day

In Puerto Rico, Christmas is celebrated for many days,
beginning on Christmas Eve and continuing until Three King's
Day on the sixth of January.

Over Hills and Valleys

(De Tierra Lejana)

Folk Song from Puerto Rico

O - ver hills and val - leys, rid - ing from a - far, ___
De tie - rra le - ja - na ve - ni - mos a ver - te;

Three ___ kings come rid - ing, fol - low - ing the star. ___
Nos sir - ve de gui - a la es - tre - lla de o - rien - te.

O love - ly star a - shin - ing in the night, ___
O bri - llan - te es - tre - lla que a nun - cias la au - ro - ra,

O won - drous star a - glow with heav'n - ly light. ___
No nos fal - te nun - ca tu luz bien - he - cho - ra.

O love - ly star a - shin - ing in the night, ___
O bri - llan - te es - tre - lla que a nun - cias la au - ro - ra,

O won - drous star a - glow with heav'n - ly light.
No nos fal - te nun - ca tu luz bien - he - cho - ra.

Happy New Year!

This old Scottish song is often sung as an expression of friendship. Americans sing it as they greet the new year.

Auld Lang Syne

Poem by Robert Burns   Traditional Scottish Tune

1. Should auld ac-quaint-ance be for-got, And nev-er brought to mind?
2. And here's a hand, my trust-y friend, And give us a hand of thine,

Should auld ac-quaint-ance be for-got, And days of auld lang syne?
We'll take a cup of kind-ness yet, For auld — lang — syne.

REFRAIN

For auld — lang — syne, my dear, For auld — lang — syne,

We'll take a cup of kind-ness yet, For auld — lang — syne.

Can You Read This?

Now read this:

Mine eyes have seen the glory of the
 coming of the Lord;
He is tramping out the vintage where the
 grapes of wrath are stored . . .

The words are easy to read, because you have learned that
the letters stand for certain sounds. You probably find the
music more difficult to read. But the written music—the notes
on the staff—also represents a group of sounds.

You can learn to read music when you learn what the written
symbols stand for. You can begin to "hear" the sound in your
mind just the way you do when you see a written word.

Begin with Rhythm

You have probably already learned that different kinds of notes
represent sounds that are longer or shorter.

Clap this pattern:

Clap this pattern. The notes come closer together.

This pattern combines the two. Clap this one:

Add a few longer notes. Clap this pattern:

Make up your own patterns for the class to perform.

More Musical Symbols

Add the musical staff ≡≡≡ and you have more information.

Now you can see and hear how long the notes last and whether they move up or down in pitch.

Here is a simple *ostinato* for a song in your book. The notes all have the same duration. The musical line moves upward and then back down.

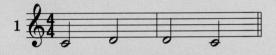

This is another ostinato for the same song. The rhythm has been changed. Clap the pattern, then read and sing it.

This ostinato pattern has a dotted rhythm and a large *leap* in the musical line.

Here is another version. The last measure is more complicated, but it is also more interesting.

Reading Longer Patterns

This melody looks complicated in the second line. However, you will find that the line moves smoothly and mostly *by step*. "Stepwise" motion is often easier to read than it looks. Each note is just next door to the one before it.

Here is a melody that *leaps*. It jumps over the notes that are next door and leaps to those further away. In this melody, the leaps get smaller and finally it ends *stepwise*.

This melody begins simply and then begins to look complicated. However, the line is almost always stepwise, and the rhythm pattern repeats. You may find it quite easy to read and sing.

You will find a *sequence* in the melody you have just read. Sequences are easy to hear and make reading music less difficult. Best of all, sequences *sound* good. Read Example 7 again and notice the sequence.

These two countermelodies will fit with a song in your book.
One is quite simple, and one is more challenging. Sing and
read the first one; then take the challenge and try the more
difficult melody.

Here is a melody that seems to swing back and forth on the same set of notes. These notes outline a *chord* you can play to accompany the song.

A Musical Map

Reading this melody is a little like taking a trip on a road you have never seen. Just follow your "map."

Now you should be ready for a longer road. If you take this melody one section at a time, you shouldn't lose your way.

This melody uses symbols and combinations you have learned to read. Now that you know how to follow a musical map and how to look for patterns, you should be able to put it together to read and sing.

A Beautiful Melody

A very familiar song will fit with this melody.

Here is a melody in a minor tonality.

Mix and Match

These short melodies can each be repeated over and over, and
sung with a song in your book. Or you can begin with
Example 16 and sing one after the other to make one long
melody.

Now that you are familiar with these melodies, invent your
own pattern for singing them with the recording.

Playing the Recorder

Using your left hand, cover the holes shown in the first diagram.

Cover the top of the mouthpiece with your lips. Blow gently as you whisper "daah." You will be playing B.

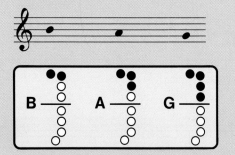

When you can play B, A, and G, you will be able to play melodies 1, 2, and 3.

Practice playing two new notes—high C and high D. When you can play them, you are ready to try melody 4.

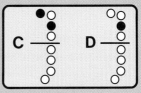

4.

Here are four new notes to practice. When you can play them, you will be ready to try melody 5.

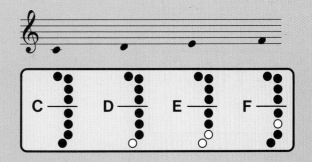

5.

Using the notes you have learned so far, you will be able to play some of the songs in your book. Try one of these.

- Zuni Sunrise Song, page 24
- Johnny Has Gone for a Soldier, page 26
- Amazing Grace, page 32
- Sweet Betsy from Pike, page 34
- Land of the Silver Birch, page 80
- Alleluia, Amen, page 108
- Oh, Be Joyful, page 172
- Chumbara, page 174
- Glory to God in the Highest, page 185
- Evening of Roses, page 194

Here are two new notes to practice—F♯ and B♭. When you can play them, you will be ready to try the melody of one of the songs listed below.

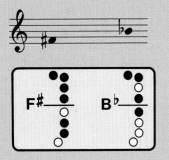

- Nine Hundred Miles, page 48
- De Colores, page 74
- Viva L'Amour, page 101
- When the Saints Go Marching In, p. 119
- Kum Ba Yah, page 127
- The Water Is Wide, page 168
- Old Abram Brown, page 189
- Jingle Bells, page 232
- The Huron Carol, page 243
- Auld Lang Syne, page 245

Playing the Guitar

This is how the neck of the guitar looks. Notice especially the parts that are labeled.

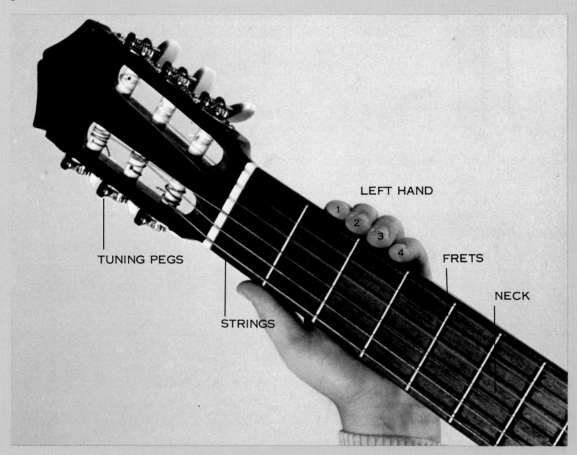

The E-Minor Chord

When you have learned to play the E-minor chord, you will be able to play an accompaniment for several songs in your book. The chord diagram shows you where to put your fingers on the strings. Press the strings and practice strumming with your thumb.

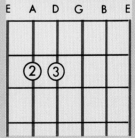

Using the fingering for the E-minor chord, strum the steady beat to accompany the following songs.

- Zum Gali Gali, page 116
- Tumba, page 182
- Old Abram Brown, page 189

The C and G₇ Chords

These chord diagrams show you how to play the C and G₇ chords.

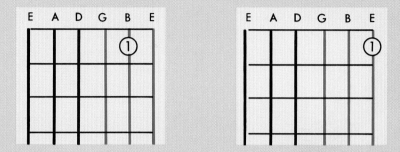

Use the C and G₇ chords to accompany "Chumbara," page 174.

Here is another song you can accompany with the C and G₇ chords.

Mary Ann

All day, all night, Ma - ry Ann,_____

Down by the sea - shore sift - ing sand._____

Ev - en lit - tle chil - dren join in the band_____

Down by the sea - shore sift - ing sand._____

Try accompanying one of the following songs by ear using the C and G₇ chords.

- He's Got the Whole World in His Hands
- Row, Row, Row Your Boat
- Goodby, Old Paint

The G and D₇ Chords

Practice changing back and forth from the G chord to the D₇ chord. Then try accompanying "Clementine" or "Old Texas."

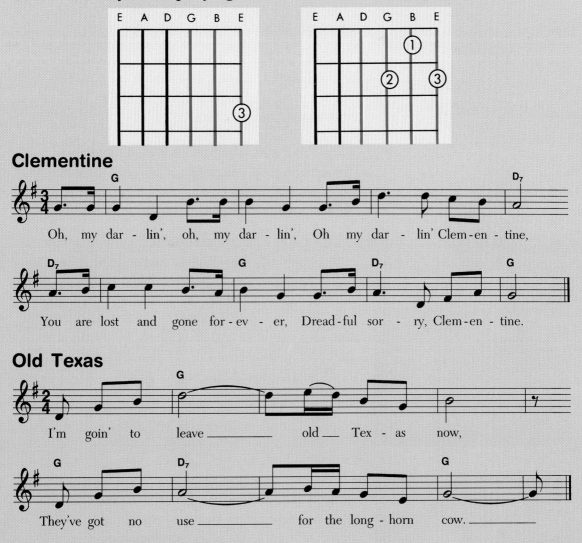

Clementine

Oh, my dar-lin', oh, my dar-lin', Oh my dar-lin' Clem-en-tine,

You are lost and gone for-ev-er, Dread-ful sor-ry, Clem-en-tine.

Old Texas

I'm goin' to leave _____ old _____ Tex-as now,

They've got no use _____ for the long-horn cow. _____

Chord Family of G (G D₇ C)

You can use the G, D₇, and C chords to accompany the following songs in your book.

The Sound Bank

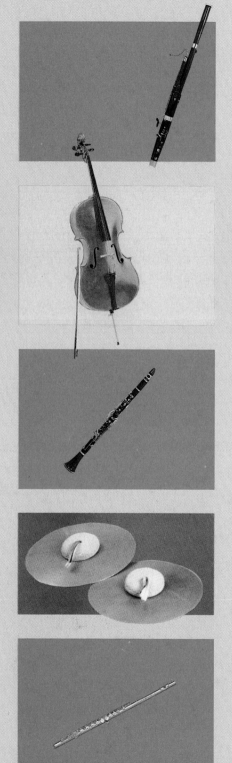

Bassoon A large, tube-shaped wooden wind instrument with a double reed and metal keys on the side. (p. 146)

• Lower notes on the bassoon may sound gruff and comical. Higher notes are the ones fifth-graders sing, and these are softer, sweeter and gentler.

Cello A large wooden string instrument which may be plucked or played with a bow. Players hold the instrument between their knees and reach around to play it. (p. 146)

• The cello has a rich-sounding, warm voice. It can make low notes, but can also reach the higher notes fifth-graders sing.

Clarinet A cylinder-shaped wind instrument, usually made of wood. There are holes and metal keys on the side of the clarinet, and a reed in the mouthpiece. (p. 92)

• Low notes on the clarinet arc soft and hollow. The middle notes are open and bright, and the highest notes are piercing.

Cymbals Two metal plates with handstraps. The player holds one cymbal in each hand and quickly claps them together. (p. 55)

• Cymbals make a loud, exciting, metallic crash when struck together.

Flute A small metal instrument shaped like a pipe, with holes and keys on its side. The player holds the flute sideways and blows across an open mouthpiece. (p. 146)

• The sound of the flute is pure, and sweet. Its low notes are the ones fifth-graders sing, but it can go much higher.

French horn A medium-sized brass instrument. At one end is a large "bell" and at the other is a funnel-shaped mouthpiece. The player holds the horn on his lap and keeps one hand inside the bell. (p. 146)

- The horn has a mellow, warm tone. Its clearest notes are the same ones fifth-graders sing, but it can also go higher and lower.

Guitar A wooden string instrument with six strings. The player strums or plucks it with a pick or the fingers to play a melody or chords. Some guitars are electric. They are flat instead of hollow, and they must be plugged into an amplifier. (p. 146)

- When played softly, the guitar is gentle and sweet. It sounds lush and powerful when it is played louder. Electric guitars can play much louder than regular guitars. They can also make many special sounds.

Oboe A slender wooden instrument with a double reed and metal keys and holes on its side. (p. 146)

- In its low voice the oboe can sound mysterious and oriental. These are the notes fifth-graders can sing. It can also play higher, thinner, sweeter notes.

Piano A large keyboard instrument with 88 keys and many strings on the inside. The player presses the keys and hammers inside the piano strike the strings to make the sound. (p. 28)

- The piano can play high and low. Many notes can be sounded at the same time.

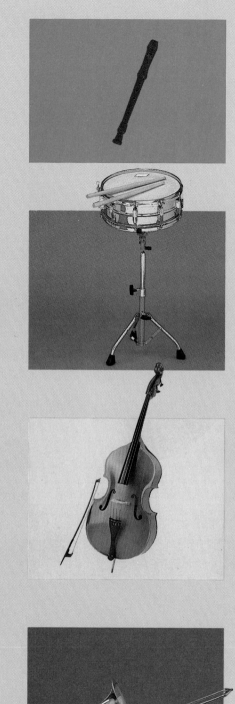

Recorder A simple wind instrument with a "whistle" mouthpiece. Recorders are made of wood or of plastic, and there are eight holes in the side. (p. 24)

- Recorders come in many sizes, with the larger ones playing lower notes. All sizes of recorders have a gentle, hollow sound.

Snare Drum A small cylinder-shaped drum. Snare drums have a flat surface on top made of calf-skin or plastic. Several thin metal coils are stretched across the bottom. The player strikes the drum with wooden sticks. (p. 38)

- Many different sounds may be made on a snare drum. It can play a steady beat or produce a raspy, rolling sound.

String Bass A very large wooden string instrument. It may be plucked with the fingers or played with a bow. The string bass is so tall that the player must stand behind it or sit on a high stool and reach around the front to play it. (p. 60)

- The deep, rich voice of the string bass is the lowest of all string instruments.

Trombone A large brass instrument with one of the loudest voices in the orchestra. The trombone is a long, narrow, curved tube with a "bell" at one end and a cup shaped mouthpiece at the other. It has a metal tube called a "slide" attached to the tubing. (p. 146)

- The trombone can project a huge, brilliant sound, but its soft voice is mellow. It can play the notes fifth-graders can sing, but can also go much lower.

Trumpet The smallest brass instrument. It has a "bell" at one end and a cup-shaped mouthpiece at the other. There are three valves, or buttons, on top. (p. 146)

- In its loudest voice, the trumpet has an important-sounding, brilliant tone. It can also sound soft, warm and sweet. Most of the trumpet notes can be sung by fifth-graders.

Tuba The largest brass instrument, with a very large bell which usually points upward. The tuba is so heavy that it may be set on a metal stand while the player sits behind it to blow into the cup-shaped mouthpiece. (p. 55)

- The tuba's low notes, the lowest of any brass instrument, are deep and dark sounding. The higher ones are hearty and warm.

Viola A wooden string instrument. It looks like a large violin, and is played in the same way. (p. 146)

- The viola sounds a lot like a violin, but it can play lower notes, and has a deeper, darker tone.

Violin A small wooden string instrument which is held under the chin. The player plays it with a bow or plucks it with the fingers. (p. 146)

- The violin has many different voices, from a beautiful "singing" quality to a bright, playful chirping sound. It can play the notes fifth-graders sing, but can go much higher as well.

Glossary

AB form (p. 128) A musical plan that has two different parts, or sections

ABA form (p. 130) A musical plan that has three sections. The first and last section are the same. The middle section is different.

accompaniment (p. 77) Music that supports the sound of the featured performer(s).

band (p. 55) A balanced group of instruments consisting of woodwinds, brass, and percussion.

beat (p. 90) A repeating pulse that can be felt in some music.

brass (p. 66) A group of wind instruments, including trumpets, French horns, and tubas, used in bands and orchestras.

cadence (p. 110) A group of chords or notes at the end of a phrase or piece that gives a feeling of pausing or finishing.

chamber music (p. 146) Music written for small groups, often having only one voice or instrument for each part, as in a string quartet.

chord (p. 126) Three or more different tones played or sung together.

coda (p. 189) A "tail" or short section added at the end of a piece of music.

composer (p. 82) A person who makes up pieces of music by putting sounds together in his or her own way.

contour (p. 124) The "shape" of a melody, made by the way it moves upward and downward in steps and leaps, and by repeated tones.

contrast (p. 129) Two or more things that are different. In music, slow is a contrast to fast; section A is a contrast to section B.

countermelody (p. 9) A melody that is played or sung at the same time as another melody.

descant (p. 122) A countermelody whose main function is to decorate the main tune, often soaring above the melody of the song.

duet (p. 142) A composition written for two performers.

dynamics (p. 148) The loudness and softness of sound (f, mf, p, mp, < > and so on).

ensemble (p. 142) A group of players or singers.

form (p. 130) The overall plan of a piece of music.

harmony (p. 116) Two or more different tones sounding at the same time.

improvisation (p. 69) Making up music as it is being performed.

interval (p. 125) The distance between tones.

introduction (p. 189) In a song, music played before the singing begins.

leap (p. 106) To move from one tone to another, skipping over the tones in between.

major scale (p. 109) An arrangement of eight tones in a scale according to the following intervals, or steps: whole, whole, half, whole, whole, whole, half.

measure (p. 90) A grouping of beats set off by bar lines.

melody (p. 104) A line of single tones that move upward, downward, or repeat.

melody pattern (p. 107) An arrangement of pitches into a small grouping, usually occurring often in a piece.

meter (p. 91) The way the beats of music are grouped, often in sets of two or in sets of three.

meter signature (p. 94) The numerical symbol, such as $\frac{2}{4}$ or $\frac{3}{4}$, that tells how many beats are in a measure (top number) and the kind of note that gets one beat (bottom number).

minor scale (p. 109) Several arrangements of eight tones in a scale, such as natural minor (whole, half, whole, whole, half, whole, whole).

mood (p. 180) The feeling that a piece of music gives. The *mood* of a lullaby is quiet and gentle.

orchestra (p. 28) A balanced group of instruments consisting of strings, woodwinds, brass, and percussion.

ostinato (p. 117) A rhythm or melody pattern that repeats.

partner songs (p. 118) Two or more different songs that can be sung at the same time to create harmony.

percussion (p. 7) A group of pitched or unpitched instruments that are played by striking with mallets, beaters, and so on, or by shaking.

phrase (p. 110) A musical "sentence." Each *phrase* expresses one thought.

quartet (p. 144) Any composition for four voices or instruments, each having a separate part.

range (p. 112) In a melody, the span from the lowest tone to the highest tone.

refrain (p. 9) The part of a song that repeats, using the same melody and words.

register (p. 112) The pitch (highness or lowness of a tone) location of a group of tones. If the group of tones are all high sounds, they are in a high *register*. If the group of tones are all low sounds, they are in a low *register*.

repeated tones (p. 106) Two or more tones in a row that have the same sound.

repetition (p. 130) Music that is the same, or almost the same, as music that was heard earlier.

rhythm pattern (p. 187) A group of long and short sounds.

rondo (p. 132) A musical form in which a section is repeated, with contrasting sections in between (such as ABACA).

round (p. 107) A follow-the-leader process in which all sing the same melody but start at different times.

scale (p. 108) An arrangement of pitches from lower to higher according to a specific pattern of intervals.

score (p. 148) Musical notation of a composition, with each of the instrumental (or vocal) parts shown in vertical alignment.

shanties (p. 6) Sailors' work songs.

steady beat (p. 90) Regular pulses.

step (p. 106) To move from one tone to another without skipping tones in between.

strings (p. 66) A term used to refer to stringed instruments that are played by bowing, plucking, or strumming.

strong beat (p. 96) The first beat in a measure.

tempo (p. 12) The speed of the beat in music.

texture (p. 185) The way melody and harmony go together: a melody alone, two or more melodies together, or a melody with chords.

theme (p. 29) An important melody that occurs several times in a piece of music.

tone color (p. 140) The special sound that makes one instrument or voice sound different from another.

trio (p. 143) Any composition for three voices or instruments, each having a separate part.

unison (p. 166) The same pitch.

variation (p. 136) Music that is repeated but changed in some important way.

woodwinds (p. 66) A term used to refer to wind instruments, now or originally made of wood.

Classified Index

Song Index

268 Reference Bank

Reference Bank 269

Acknowledgments

Credit and appreciation are due publishers and copyright owners for use of the following:

"Beauty" from I AM A PUEBLO INDIAN GIRL by E-Yeh-Shure. Copyright © 1939 by William Morrow & Co., Inc. Renewed 1967 by Louise Abeita Chiwiwi. By permission of William Morrow & Company.

"How Gray the Rain" from FIVE BUSHEL FARM by Elizabeth Coatsworth. Reprinted by permission of Macmillan Publishing Company. Copyright 1939 by Macmillan Publishing Company. Renewed 1967 by Elizabeth Coatsworth Beston.

"In Retreat Among Bamboos" from THE JADE MOUNTAIN: A CHINESE ANTHOLOGY, translated by Witter Bynner from the texts of Kiang Kang-Hu. Copyright 1926 and renewed 1954 by Alfred A. Knopf, Inc.

"Long Trip" from SELECTED POEMS BY LANGSTON HUGHES by Langston Hughes. Copyright 1926 by Alfred A. Knopf Inc. and renewed 1954 by Langston Hughes. Reprinted by permission of Alfred A. Knopf, Inc.

"A Song of Always" from NOW WE BEGIN by Marian J. and Efraim M. Rosenzweig.

"Washington" by Nancy Byrd Turner.

Picture Credits

Contributing Artists: Katherine Ace; Don Dyen; Gretchen Shields; Arvis Stewart; Walt Sturrock; David Wenzel; David Wisniewski.

Photographs: 4: l. Elizabeth Crews/Stock, Boston; m. Ellis Herwig/Stock, Boston; r. Imagery for Silver Burdett & Ginn. 13: Ray Manley/Shostal Associates. 15: Silver Burdett & Ginn. 16: I. N. Phelps Stokes Collection, The New York Public Library, Astor, Lenox and Tilden Foundations. 21: Silver Burdett & Ginn. 28: Bettmann Archive. 30: © George E. Jones III/Photo Researchers, Inc. 33: Silver Burdett & Ginn. 36: E. R. Degginger. 37: Silver Burdett & Ginn. 42: Julius Fekete/Taurus Photos. 43: Robert Frerck/Odyssey Productions. 44: © John Messina/Photo Researchers, Inc. 49: t.r. Lynn Goldsmith/LGI; m.l. Ron Wolfson/LGI; m.r. Richard Pasley/LGI; b. Peter Simon/LGI. 55: © Jan Halasha/Photo Researchers, Inc. 56: Brown Brothers. 61: Silver Burdett & Ginn. 64–65: Slick Lawson for Silver Burdett & Ginn; except 64: t.r. Walter Iooss, Jr./Sports Illustrated © TIME, INC. 66: Silver Burdett & Ginn. 69: Leon V. Kofod. 80: S. J. Krasemann/Peter Arnold, Inc. 82: The Art Museum of the Ateneum, Helsinki, Finland. 114: Isabella Stewart Gardner Museum, Boston/Art Resource, NY. 116: Hiroji Kubota/Magnum. 136: Silver Burdett & Ginn. 138: Deutsches Fotothek, Dresden, West Germany. 145: Silver Burdett & Ginn. 147: t. Bettmann Archive; b. The Metropolitan Museum of Art, NY, Arthur H. Hearn Fund, 1942. 152–153. Bob Kalmbach for Silver Burdett & Ginn. 166: Bettmann Archive. 173: Silver Burdett & Ginn. 174: Ed Cooper/Shostal Associates. 181: Robert Frerck/Odyssey Productions. 184: Silver Burdett & Ginn. 186: t. Richard Braaten; b. Fletcher Drake/Kennedy Center. 191: National Gallery of Art, Washington. 230: © George Holton/Photo Researchers, Inc. 233, 236: Silver Burdett & Ginn. 240: Sherry Beck/Concordia College, Ann Arbor, MI. 246: Silver Burdett & Ginn. Sound Bank Photographs: Silver Burdett & Ginn and John Bacchus, courtesy of Yamaha International Corporation, Buena Park, California; Dorn & Kirschner Band Instrument Co., Union, New Jersey; and the Morris School District, Board of Education, Morristown, New Jersey.

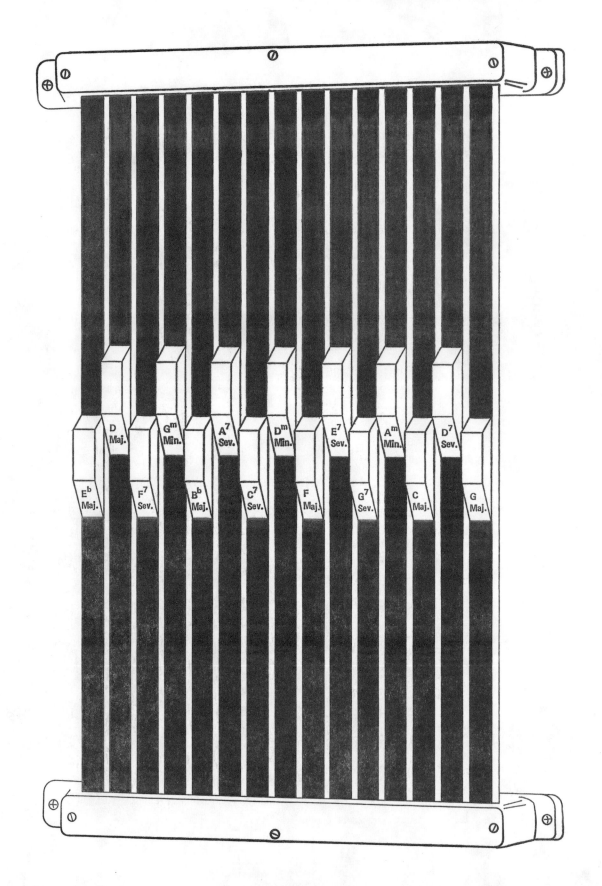